MOUNTAIN BIKE FITNESS TRAINING

MOUNTAIN BIKE FITNESS TRAINING

John Metcalfe

MAINSTREAM
PUBLISHING
EDINBURGH AND LONDON

To my parents
for their unwavering support
and enthusiasm

This edition, 2004

First published in Great Britain in 2001 by
MAINSTREAM PUBLISHING COMPANY (EDINBURGH) LTD
7 Albany Street
Edinburgh EH1 3UG

ISBN 1 84018 858 8

A catalogue record for this book is available from the British Library

Typeset in Futurist and Stone
Printed and bound in Great Britain by
Creative Print Design, Wales

Acknowledgements

This book would not have been possible without the help of several key people. Thank you; you know who you are.

Contents

Preface

Mountain biking has come a long way since its inception back in the early '70s. Once considered an alternative form of recreation, it has undergone a renaissance period, and has emerged as an Olympic sport where the stars of mountain biking battle for top honours on the world stage. A lot has changed. Few of the current top riders can master every discipline of the sport, as was so often the case in yesteryear. No longer do the stars compete in the downhill, dual slalom, and trials on the Saturday, then race to glory in the cross-country on the Sunday.

Mountain bike equipment has evolved at such a pace that the bikes used in the various disciplines are as far removed from each other as a rally car is from a Formula-One racing car. A cross-country mountain bike would barely last a minute on the world downhill circuit, and a downhill steed would be totally unsuitable for a cross-country race.

Without a doubt mountain biking has become specialised, and has done so in a diminutive time-scale. Equipment has evolved that is specific to the task; and riders have been forced to specialise. It is no longer possible to be cycling fit, put in a hard ride, and have a fair chance of doing well. Each discipline has risen to a level where the fitness and intellectual demands placed on the competitors requires total dedication and application in training, with very little room for crossover.

A popular analogy in coaching circles equates matching the fitness of a rider to a specific discipline with matching a Lottery ticket to the winning numbers. Five numbers and the bonus will not win – only all six numbers bring you the top prize. Of course, the main difference with mountain bike fitness is that it is not all down to luck. You need hard work, dedication and an intelligent training programme to succeed.

This book is a compilation of modern mountain bike training theories and philosophies designed to enable you to construct your own training plan. The information that I offer in this book has evolved from sports science research, anecdotal evidence and personal experience. All these constructs are based on contemporary information and, by their very nature, they are transient and are subject to change and interpretation. Because this is a continually evolving project, I welcome any feedback and comments from you, the reader.

John Metcalfe MSc

PART ONE

Introduction

1. FIT FOR WHAT?

– Definitions of fitness
– Components of mountain bike fitness
– Energy production

2. FITNESS ASSESSMENT AND GOAL-SETTING

– Identifying weak fitness areas
– The role of fitness testing
– Goal-setting

3. TRAINING PRINCIPLES

– Overload and supercompensation
– Progressive overload
– Over-training
– Specificity
– Reversibility
– Variety

1. FIT FOR WHAT?

DEFINITIONS OF FITNESS

The phrase 'I'm going to have to get fitter' gets used a lot during the mountain bike race season. This is especially so after a particularly gruelling race, or towards the end of a race series when most riders have been put through their paces. We have all used the phrase ourselves at one time or another, but what exactly do we mean by getting fitter? And, more importantly, how do you go about getting fit?

Well, fitness can be a very intractable term to define because it is intricately woven into the fabric of our everyday speech. Fitness has multiple meanings, ranging from the widespread understanding of being in suitable condition to perform a task, to a more depressing clinical interpretation of being defined as a distance from death.

Even putting these mainstream definitions aside, within the sport of mountain biking there is much contention about the understanding of the concept. Different riders have different interpretations. What an Expert class rider regards as fitness differs greatly from that of a Fun class rider (see chapter seventeen). But on the whole, getting fit boils down to the same thing: being able to ride faster for longer.

For the purpose of this book, I shall apply the sports science interpretation of the term fitness, and will focus mainly upon the physical and skill-related properties of a rider. The components of fitness that are required in mountain biking are summarised in table 1. However, the mental fitness of a rider can often be the determining factor between racing success and failure because it orchestrates all of the other fitness components. It is important that we have an understanding of each of these components and what its specific role in mountain biking is.

Table 1: Components of Mountain Bike Fitness

PHYSICAL		SKILL
Strength	Aerobic Power	Agility
Speed	Flexibility	Co-ordination
Anaerobic Power	Body Composition	Balance
Muscular Endurance		Reaction Time

COMPONENTS OF MOUNTAIN BIKE FITNESS

Physical Fitness

When riders talk about having to get fit, it is usually the physical aspects of fitness that they are referring to. This is the area of fitness that most mountain bikers associate with improved performance, and the individual components that comprise physical fitness are discussed below.

STRENGTH Scientifically speaking, strength is the ability of a muscle, or a group of muscles, to generate a force against a resistance. Maximal, or absolute, strength refers to the maximum amount of force a muscle can exert over a short period of time. Whilst this may be of major importance in weight lifting, it is rarely a factor in mountain biking. Of greater relevance to your mountain bike performance is your ability to generate dynamic strength. Dynamic strength is concerned with being strong over a prolonged period of time. The peak force that is generated is considerably less than that during a maximal strength exertion, but it can be sustained for longer. You will be calling on your dynamic strength when you are sprinting for the holeshot, or are cranking your way up a steep climb.

SPEED In its literal sense, the speed component of your fitness is concerned with the rate at which you are able to complete the distance of the course. The quicker the time it takes you, the faster you are. However, speed is also related to how quickly you can set your limbs in motion. If you have a fast leg speed you will be able to generate high cadences, which in turn will also be a determining factor in your ability to accelerate quickly.

ANAEROBIC POWER Anaerobic power is the maximum rate at which you can generate energy from your anaerobic systems. In mountain biking, anaerobic power is used to sustain highly intense activity such as the starting sprint, or it can be used in explosive movements such as jumps and bunny hops. Downhill mountain biking and dual slalom require a high degree of anaerobic power.

MUSCULAR ENDURANCE Muscular endurance is the capacity of a muscle to contract repeatedly without fatiguing. In order to turn the cranks continually throughout a cross-country race, you will need a high degree of muscular endurance.

AEROBIC POWER Aerobic power (often called aerobic work capacity) is the rate at which you can produce energy from your aerobic energy system. As the name suggests, aerobic power requires the presence of oxygen, and is highly dependent on the efficiency of your cardiovascular system. If this component is highly developed you will be able to maintain a fast pace for a prolonged period of time without lactic acid accumulating.

FLEXIBILITY Flexibility is concerned with the range of movement in a joint. Upon first appraisal the role of flexibility in mountain biking may appear to be limited – and as such it is often overlooked – this is not the case. Flexibility, as we shall see in subsequent chapters, is a significant mountain bike fitness component and can contribute greatly to the efficiency and safety of a rider.

BODY COMPOSITION Body composition refers to the relative percentages of body fat and lean muscle tissue. To enhance your cycling efficiency, you should aim to maximise your lean tissue whilst minimising your body fat.

Skill-Related Fitness

Skill-related fitness is an area often overlooked when fitness training is discussed colloquially. However, the skill components are a legitimate aspect of mountain bike fitness. After all, there is no point being super fit in a physical sense if you can't ride your mountain bike efficiently.

AGILITY Agility is a product of co-ordination, balance and reaction time. It is concerned with being able to alter the position of your body very quickly and accurately without losing your balance. All mountain bike disciplines require this component to a high degree, but none more so than dual slalom, where obstacles and other riders must be avoided.

CO-ORDINATION Co-ordination in mountain biking is concerned with being able to orchestrate each of your body parts in order to produce accurate, flawless skills. For some lucky riders co-ordination seems to be innate; fortunately, for those other mere mortals, co-ordination can be learnt and improved with practice.

BALANCE In its simplest sense, balance is about being able to stay on two wheels without falling over. As a mountain biker, your ability to balance is aided greatly by your momentum and the gyroscopic effects of your wheels. In other words if you ride fast you'll have a greater chance of staying upright. However, this is not the complete story because a large amount of skill is also required in order to maintain a stable position, especially when you are riding slowly or on undulating terrain.

REACTION TIME Reaction time is concerned with how quickly you respond to a stimulus. In mountain biking there many stimuli to respond to – trees, roots, rocks and other riders, to name but a few. Each one of these stimuli has many possible responses and, as such, choices have to made. Therefore reaction time also involves decision making, and this has been found to be greatly influenced by experience.

It follows that in order to 'get fit' each one of your fitness components must be enhanced and honed to the extent that it matches the fitness requirements of your chosen mountain bike discipline. No matter how advanced some of your fitness components are, you will only be as good as your weakest component, so the process of getting fit is a juggling act where you must continually keep working on every aspect of your fitness. Unfortunately, this process of improvement cannot go on indefinitely. Each of us has a predetermined, maximum level for each component as determined by our genes. To reach your genetic potential is an arduous task to say the least, and as you strive to improve your mountain bike fitness you will be continually hampered by other constraining factors. Your main adversary is going to be your ability to produce energy.

ENERGY PRODUCTION

Even if you have reached the envious condition of having all of your fitness components harmoniously operating at their ceiling limits, all is not done. Your body's systems need energy to function properly: no matter how well developed they are, if they don't get the correct amount of energy at the appropriate time they will grind to a halt. Ultimately the energy used to fuel these systems comes from the food that you eat, and your ability to extract the chemical energy from food can determine how well you are going to race. It really can be as simple as that.

The nutrient energy 'locked up' in your food cannot be used directly by your working muscles. Instead it must be converted, by a chemical process called respiration, to adenosine triphosphate (ATP). This comprises an adenosine molecule with three phosphates attached to it via energy-rich bonds. The energy released when these bonds are broken is then used to power the muscular contractions that you make. Humans are only able to store a limited amount of ATP, and as such it can only supply the energy for a few seconds of physical activity. Therefore ATP must be continually re-synthesised.

There are three ways that your body can continually re-synthesise ATP whilst you are exercising, these are:

PHOSPHOCREATINE SYSTEM The muscles also store phosphocreatine (PC) which is another chemical compound with energy rich bonds. The energy yielded when PC is metabolised is used to re-synthesise ATP. Once again the stores of PC are also limited and can only contribute about another three to four seconds of physical activity before becoming depleted. Obviously mountain bike races last longer than several seconds, so your body will switch to another system to produce energy – anaerobic glycolysis.

ANAEROBIC GLYCOLYSIS Anaerobic glycolysis is the process whereby nutrient energy from the metabolism of carbohydrates is used to re-synthesise ATP. In order to yield energy relatively quickly, this process is performed anaerobically (without oxygen). As a result the carbohydrate is not fully metabolised and lactic acid is the by-product. Every mountain biker should be familiar with the sensations associated with lactic acid accumulation; it is that burning feeling in your thighs just after you have done a hard sprint. Anaerobic glycolysis contributes to the energy equation for relatively intense exercise lasting several minutes, for example when you attempt to lose a competitor by increasing the pace for several minutes.

If your mountain biking is to continue for longer than several minutes, your body will produce energy from the final system – aerobic glycolysis.

AEROBIC GLYCOLYSIS Aerobic glycolysis involves the complete metabolism of food and requires the presence of oxygen. The maximum amount of energy is released and there is no lactic acid produced. The price of this efficiency is a slower energy turnover than that of anaerobic glycolysis. Because of this, if you wish to ride for long periods, you must accommodate a reduction in your pace. Aerobic glycolysis is a significant contributor of energy when you are competing in a cross country race, and it is also the energy system of choice in ultra-distance events and expedition touring.

It is therefore the availability of both oxygen and substrate (fuel) to the working muscles that is the major limiting factor in your ability to produce energy. If there is not enough oxygen present and lactic acid is allowed to accumulate in your muscles you will fatigue prematurely and your performance will suffer. This occurs when you sprint as fast as you can, for example at the start of a race. Here you will be exercising anaerobically, and as you know you cannot keep this pace up for very long. Pretty soon you have two options: either slow down the pace so that you can meet your body's oxygen demands, or continue at this pace for a short while and then grind to a complete halt.

The solution is not just a case of breathing in more air, absorbing more oxygen and therefore getting fitter. Instead there is a long chain of events that occur between your breathing in air, and oxygen arriving at your exercising leg muscles. As you inhale, air is drawn into the lungs. Then, during the process of gaseous exchange, oxygen has to combine with your red blood cells. The blood is then pumped to your working muscles by your heart and thence through the body. The oxygen from the blood then has to be extracted by the working muscles. Oxygen absorption and utilisation is thus dependent upon the efficiency of your lungs, the ability of your blood to carry oxygen, the ability of your heart to pump the blood, and the efficiency of your muscle fibres.

The maximum volume of oxygen that you are able to absorb and use is called your VO_2 max. It is measured in ml/kg of bodyweight/minute. In mountain biking circles, this value has become synonymous with fitness: if rider A has a greater VO_2 maximum than rider B, Rider A is often considered to be the fitter. But as we shall see in subsequent chapters, this is a misconception because VO_2 max is really only a measure of your fitness potential.

It follows that a deficiency in any of the many links in the above chain will drastically reduce your potential capacity to produce energy. It is apparent that a number of the constricting factors are beyond your control, and you can therefore do little about them. What you can do, however, is aim to accentuate each of the links that you can influence, and the only vehicle that can help you achieve this goal is the appropriate type of training.

2. FITNESS ASSESSMENT AND GOAL-SETTING

IDENTIFYING WEAK FITNESS AREAS

If we examine the riding abilities of any mountain bike champion we can see that they have no weak areas – just strong ones. This is because mountain bike performance is the result of an elaborate chain of fitness components that all act together synergistically. Your overall mountain bike performance is not just the sum of these separate abilities. In the same way that a chain is only as strong as its weakest link, you are only as good as your worst ability.

Research has shown that, when left to their own devices, most athletes avoid training their weak areas because they are no good at them. Instead, human nature being what it is, they train their strong areas because it makes them feel good. The net result is that their strengths get stronger and their weaknesses weaker. Unfortunately, one does not necessarily offset the other. For example, if your forte is climbing, then being extra good at climbing is not going to make up for poor endurance in a race. You simply will not last the course. In this instance, you would be better off focusing your efforts on bringing your weak link up to par.

Small changes in your weak areas will have a great effect on your overall performance, while making a significant improvement in your strongest areas will have a diminished effect. Therefore when devising your training programme, you must first of all identify your weakest areas and make them your number-one training priority. Focusing on your weaknesses is not a negative approach. Once you have highlighted your troublesome fitness components, it is like discovering that you have been driving around with your handbrake on. Once you've realised this, you can release the brake that has blighted your progress, and reap the benefits.

Identifying, learning about and monitoring your weak points is half the battle in mountain bike training. Before you begin to design your mountain bike training programme, it is imperative that you have your fitness level assessed. Fitness assessment tests are an integral part of any mountain bike training plan, as they allow a snapshot of your fitness status at a particular point in time. Pre-training fitness tests give you an overview of your initial fitness level, which, if compared to the fitness demands of the sport, will highlight your weak areas. You can then use this information to design your yearly training programme.

Diagram 1 illustrates a hypothetical situation where a rider has undergone several tests to assess the status of a number of fitness components. Clearly components A and C are weak areas and require attention, whereas component B is a strong area and should be maintained.

Diagram 1: Comparing Desired and Actual Fitness Levels

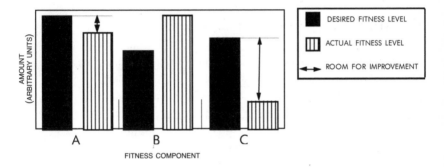

THE ROLE OF FITNESS TESTING

In order to ascertain the fitness demands of mountain biking you need to analyse the fitness components of riders who are better than you. If you are nearing the upper echelons of mountain biking, it would be useful for you to obtain fitness data for professional riders. This is often a lot easier said than done, as data like this is usually a closely guarded secret. An alternative approach is to contact the British Cycling Federation (BCF) and ask for a copy of their selection criteria for fitness tests. You can then use this as a yardstick and see how you measure up. If, however, you have not yet reached such dizzy heights in your mountain bike career, a more practical approach would be to assess those riders who are performing well in your race category. Once again, you may find that riders are a bit cagey about broadcasting their fitness data because they don't want to give anything away. However, if you are a member of a good mountain bike club, the more experienced riders are often more than willing to lend a helpful hand and share whatever information you need.

Testing also serves an important role during your training programme, as it provides you with valuable feedback about how you are progressing (or, just as importantly, if you're not). If you are on course then this confirmation is an all-important confidence boost. If your training is not going as planned, the test results will highlight which areas in your training programme need altering in order to bring about the desired effect.

Fitness testing need not mean white coats and laboratories. In fact, anything you use to assess your fitness can be classified as a test. For example, you may perform a ten-mile time trial as part of your training, or enter the same race each month, and compare the results over time to see if you are getting any better. This anecdotal approach is fine for getting a 'feel' for how things are going; but can you be sure that the reason why you got a better result this time was due to an increased fitness and not because there was a tailwind this week? Or because less people turned up for the race this month? You must also be sure that you know exactly which aspect of your fitness you are trying to assess.

For this reason it is best to use validated and reliable tests rather than make up your own. Without a doubt the most accurate fitness tests are those performed in laboratories, but what they gain in accuracy they can lose on sport specificity. They can also be expensive and inconvenient. It is possible to get a free laboratory assessment by contacting your local university Exercise Physiology department and offering your services as a guinea pig. Exercise Physiology undergraduates are always looking for subjects to test and will no doubt be glad of your call.

A compromise between accuracy and sports specificity does exist. Field-test equivalents of the laboratory tests have been designed which have the best of both worlds: they are sport specific whilst maintaining a good degree of accuracy. Throughout this book, where appropriate, I have included the relevant testing protocols.

You should ensure that you perform your fitness tests under similar conditions every time (same venue, weather conditions, time of day, etc.) as this will reduce the number of uncontrollable variables and render your tests more accurate. Also try to make things equal within yourself by ensuring you get enough rest, and that you have adequate glycogen stores for the tests.

Due to their nature, fitness tests are physically demanding and as such care must be taken to ensure that they do not detract from your training. Use them sparingly and substitute them with the corresponding workout in order to avoid over-training. The proof is in the pudding, as they say, and a great deal of information about your weak areas can be gleaned from a post-race analysis. Below is a questionnaire, based on a Likert scale, which you should complete after each race. The results from this should be in accordance with your physical fitness tests, but they may also unearth other weaknesses that are not always apparent until you are put in a race scenario.

By definition you cannot have weak spots in all areas. You may have one or two areas holding you back which are relatively weak compared to your other abilities. Concentrate on making these weaknesses your future strengths. Be smart: work on these areas until you feel your efforts would gain greater results if you applied them to another aspect of your mountain biking training.

Table 2: Fitness Assessment Questionnaire

SCORING THE QUESTIONNAIRE:
Rate your ability in each category on the corresponding scale using the following key:

> 5 – strongly agree
> 4 – agree
> 3 – neutral
> 2 – disagree
> 1 – strongly disagree

Compute the scores for each component. The range for each component is from 4 (very weak) to 20 (very strong) with the average being 12. Rate each of the components to assess your strong and weak areas.

VERY WEAK		WEAK			BELOW AVERAGE		AVERAGE			ABOVE AVERAGE		STRONG			VERY STRONG	
4	5	6	7	8	9	10	11	12	13	14	15	16	17	18	19	20

COMPONENT: ANAEROBIC THRESHOLD / LACTATE TOLERANCE
During the race . . .

When I performed repeated sprints, my last sprint was as good as my first	— 5 — 4 — 3 — 2 — 1 —
I recovered quickly after sprinting hard	— 5 — 4 — 3 — 2 — 1 —
I regularly out-sprinted other riders	— 5 — 4 — 3 — 2 — 1 —
When I was sprinting 'all out' my pace was constant and didn't taper off	— 5 — 4 — 3 — 2 — 1 —

COMPONENT: ENDURANCE
During the race . . .

I perform better than if it were run over a shorter distance	— 5 — 4 — 3 — 2 — 1 —
I overtook more people during the latter part of the race than overtook me	— 5 — 4 — 3 — 2 — 1 —
I did not feel daunted by the length of the race	— 5 — 4 — 3 — 2 — 1 —
I did not feel weak towards the end	— 5 — 4 — 3 — 2 — 1 —

COMPONENT: CLIMBING (CROSS-COUNTRY SPECIFIC)

During the race . . .

I overtook more people on the climbs than overtook me	— 5 — 4 — 3 — 2 — 1 —
I recovered quickly after climbing hard	— 5 — 4 — 3 — 2 — 1 —
I performed best on the climbs	— 5 — 4 — 3 — 2 — 1 —
On longer climbs, my pace is constant and doesn't taper off	— 5 — 4 — 3 — 2 — 1 —

COMPONENT: POWER

During the race . . .

I was with the leaders at the start	— 5 — 4 — 3 — 2 — 1 —
I recover quickly after explosive hard sprints	— 5 — 4 — 3 — 2 — 1 —
I was able to 'honk' up short steep hills	— 5 — 4 — 3 — 2 — 1 —
I was able to drop riders over short distances	— 5 — 4 — 3 — 2 — 1 —

COMPONENT: SKILLS/ERGONOMICS

During the race . . .

I made very few gear selection errors	— 5 — 4 — 3 — 2 — 1 —
I did not fall off very often	— 5 — 4 — 3 — 2 — 1 —
I was faster on the tight tricky single track than most other riders	— 5 — 4 — 3 — 2 — 1 —
I enjoyed the tight turns, drop-offs, and negotiating obstacles	— 5 — 4 — 3 — 2 — 1 —

GOAL-SETTING

The road to fitness can be an undulating one, littered with numerous blind alleys and cul-de-sacs. But as with any journey, life is made far easier with a clearly defined destination and a map showing the quickest possible way to get there. Despite the well-documented advantages of having a game plan to adhere to, anecdotal evidence suggests that very few mountain bikers actually have a tangible goal that they can work towards. This lack of direction invariably leads to a 'hit-and-miss' approach to training and results in a lot of misguided time and effort.

If you have followed the above advice and have identified your weak links, then you are halfway to setting yourself appropriate training goals. But, before you put any physical effort into your mountain bike training, it is wise to assess exactly what it is you want to achieve, and clearly define your goals. Sports psychology research suggests a set of criteria that a goal must meet in order for it to be fully effective. The criteria are as follows:

Specific
Your goals must be clearly defined. This single factor cannot be overstated. You should know exactly what it is you are working towards; preferably you should also include a realistic timescale. Just wanting to get fitter, or win a race is too nebulous. Your goals need to be tangible. Wanting to lose two kilograms of bodyweight within a month is an example of a specific goal.

Improvement
To be worthwhile, your fitness goals should be based on continual improvement, rather than just maintaining your current performance.

Controllable
It is important that you have control over your goals if they are to be effective. Wanting to beat another rider is not a controllable goal; it is outcome orientated, greatly influenced by the other rider. Even if you were to attain this goal, you have no way of knowing whether it was due to your increased fitness levels or whether the other rider just had a bad race. Of course, success in mountain bike racing is all about being victorious, and no doubt your principal goal will be to attain a certain ranking in relation to other riders. This is fine, but you must also ensure that your fitness goals along the way are controllable and relevant to you. Make them performance related.

Challenging
Setting yourself an easy goal will give you very little reward and satisfaction. Similarly, unrealistic, difficult goals will be the cause of much aggravation. You should therefore set yourself practical goals which are a challenge to achieve.

Attainable
It follows then that your goals must be attainable. If you set yourself the sole task of winning the World Championships before you have even won a Sports class (see chapter seventeen) race, then it will no doubt be the cause of much disappointment. It is fine to want to climb to the summit of Everest; just be sure to make base camps on the way up. Make your goals as difficult as possible, yet attainable with effort.

Measurable
It is important that you have some way of measuring whether or not you have been

successful at achieving your goal. You must therefore have clearly defined objectives from the outset. Just wanting to be fitter is not a measurable goal, for you need to state quantitatively the level of fitness that you wish to achieve. Fitness diagnostic tests are excellent tools for measuring your goals.

Personal
Your goals must be specific to you. You should set yourself personal goals that are not unduly influenced by the performance of others. You should also bear in mind that, longitudinally, your goals are transient and will change. Your goals for now will no doubt change over time as you successively attain them.

It is also a good idea to stratify your goals in to three levels, as highlighted below:

Level I
These are the goals that you should be able to achieve. Here you might include the basic fitness level that you should be able to reach unless something goes awry.

Level II
These are the goals that you could achieve it you truly worked at them. These are your main goals that are attainable with effort. If you have more than one goal then you should prioritise them.

Level III
These are the goals that are possible, and that you just might achieve if everything goes your way. Don't make these unrealistic – remember, they must still be possible.

Once you have decided upon your goals, write them down. This is a big step. Your goals have now changed from an abstract idea to something that is tangible. For the first time, you now have evidence of the mountain bike goals that you wish to achieve. Your next step is to set yourself a realistic timescale for achieving them. Again, be specific and write down the actual date. For your primary mountain bike goal this date will probably be synonymous with the date of your most important race. However you should also include timescales for your other goals. To complete the goal-setting procedure, you should also write down a plan of how you are going to achieve them. This final step is dealt with in greater detail in chapter eight.

As you can see, the philosophy behind goal-setting is that it is a dynamic and ever-changing process: what is a goal now may need to be modified in a month or two when you achieve it. In order to keep progressing, you must constantly assess your abilities and alter your goals accordingly.

3. TRAINING PRINCIPLES

OVERLOAD AND SUPERCOMPENSATION

Now that you have established your weak areas and clearly defined your training goals, the next step is to apply the principles of training. The basic concept behind any training programme is to make your body perform more exercise than it is accustomed to. For mountain biking this involves riding further (duration), more often (frequency), or faster (intensity) than normal, or a combination of all three. Increasing the exercise like this is termed 'overload'. Overloading in this manner puts greater stress on your body than usual and causes your metabolic and biological systems to work at maximal or near maximal efforts.

As a result of overload your body upgrades, or adapts, to the new workload and becomes more efficient. When this adaptation has occurred, the exercise is said to have initiated a training response. Sports scientists call this upgrading 'supercompensation' (A in diagram 2), and it allows you to perform more work for the same amount of effort, or the same work with less effort. Put another way: you have become fitter.

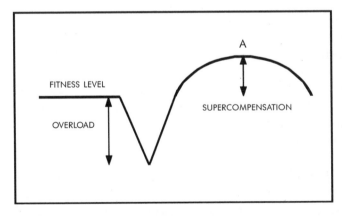

Diagram 2: Overload and Supercompensation

PROGRESSIVE OVERLOAD

If you so wished you could leave it there and rest on your laurels; however, a properly designed mountain bike programme will incorporate progressive overload. Progressive overload is the same principle as overload, except that at the peak of supercompensation you should increase the workload again, which causes further adaptation. This should continue until you reach your maximum mountain bike potential. In theory it sounds easy, but in practice it can be a different story.

Diagram 3: Progressive Overload

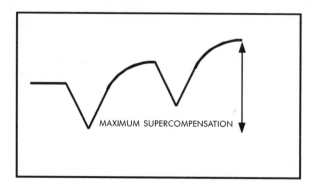

MAXIMUM SUPERCOMPENSATION

Diagrammatically, progressive overload is an easy concept to understand. However, when it comes to transferring the principle to a real-life training situation, problems arise. The issue is not with the progressive overload principle per se, but how it is used and applied. People think, 'If this much exercise is making me this much fitter, then twice as much exercise will make me twice as fit, right?' WRONG!

Your body does not get fit when you are riding your mountain bike. In fact it only supercompensates or adapts when you are resting, so recovery periods should be built into every mountain bike training programme. If you regularly overload your body and do not allow time for adequate recovery and adaptation to occur, you are running the risk of over-training.

OVER-TRAINING

Over-training is a widely used term and is all too often used generically to explain poor performance. There are in fact two precursor conditions before a state of over-training is actually reached.

The first stage is called 'overload' as described above. If insufficient rest occurs, it is quickly followed by the second stage, which is termed 'over-reaching'. Characteristic symptoms of over-reaching are a noticeable deterioration in your mountain bike performance, and a persistent feeling that you are not operating at 100 per cent. These symptoms are sometimes hard to detect – riders can easily shrug them off, just thinking they are having a 'bad week' – but once they are recognised, a return to form is possible following a few days of complete rest. Unfortunately the typical knee-jerk reaction to these symptoms is the belief that more training will kick-start the training progression. Of course this just stirs up the muddied waters and facilitates the onset of the full-blown condition of over-training.

Diagram 4: Over-training

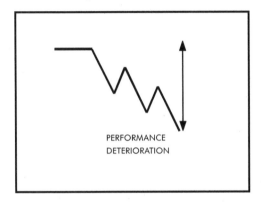

PERFORMANCE
DETERIORATION

The problem is not knowing when you are at the height of supercompensation, and therefore when you should start your subsequent exercise bout. Initiate your next workout after supercompensation has occurred and you will not be improving your fitness at your optimal rate. Initiate it too early and you run the risk of over-training. It is a fine line that you have to tread, and the only way to learn is through experience, trial and error, and careful monitoring of your recovery status.

Both mentally and physically, over-training is a severe form of fatigue, with the only cure being complete rest. Ironically, the condition is brought about by the same three factors that improve performance: training for too long, training too often, or training too hard. Nine times out of ten, it is the latter situation that leads to over-training in mountain bikers. This is because a lot of mountain bikers don't know how to 'train easy'. As you shall see later in this book, easy training days are an integral component of a mountain biker's training programme. Easy days – or active recovery days, as they are known – are necessary in order to facilitate the recovery process. When performing training at this easy intensity, a lot of riders fall into the trap of thinking that it is of no benefit to them, and if they are to salvage anything from the workout then they are going to have to up the ante. This is a recipe for disaster. With an increase in intensity, and a subsequent reduction in recovery, over-training is a certainty.

Because there is such a fine line between maximal improvement and over-training, a lot of mountain bikers are over-trained. Typical indications of over-training include: a lack of improvement in mountain bike performance despite continued training; a lack of appetite; insomnia; elevated morning heart rate; general lethargy; persistent colds; lingering muscle soreness; poor concentration; and a lack of motivation.

To make things difficult, it is quite normal for any one of these symptoms to be present during a non-over-trained period without requiring cause for concern. What you must be alert for is the continued presence of a combination of these ailments, or a continuous change in your normal condition. As a rule of thumb, if you suspect you are over-training, back off for a few days and see if your energy, motivation and performance improve. If they do, take a further week off training (more if necessary) in order to complete the recovery process fully, and when you return to your training keep a keen eye on your recovery status. Remember: if in doubt, rest.

SPECIFICITY

The specificity principle refers to the particular biological effects that a certain method of training has. It follows, then, that sprint training initiates certain adaptations which are different from those brought about by long-distance rides and vice versa. Similarly, a weight-training programme for your legs will not increase the muscle bulk of your arms. This may sound like common sense, but there are an awful lot of riders who go out on a 'training ride' not knowing exactly what it is they are working on.

The point to bear in mind when you are designing your training programme is that training is not a 'hit-and-miss' affair; you can't just go out for a ride and get fit. Because specific training methods initiate specific training changes, you should know exactly what fitness component you are targeting and then train accordingly.

REVERSIBILITY

The dictum 'if you don't use it, you'll lose it' underpins the reversibility principle. De-training occurs when the training adaptations are reversed or lost due to a period of reduced training or inactivity. Research has shown that significant decreases occur after only one or two weeks' inactivity. This reversal is an in-built primal function that has evolved over the millennia to ensure that our bodies are thrifty and operate at their most economical level. From a survival perspective, there is no point servicing and maintaining extra tissues if they are not needed; they are a waste of precious resources. So in order to get fit and build new tissue, we must justify their existence through hard training.

The important ramifications of this principle are that training changes are therefore transient and reversible. This means that you must still train, even if you only want to maintain your fitness, and the fitter you get the harder it becomes to initiate a training response.

VARIETY

The bottom line is that boredom kills training. It is the major reason why riders quit training programmes. No matter how motivated you are, if the training programme is repetitive and uninteresting then your enthusiasm will wane and your fitness level will stagnate or even deteriorate. You should enjoy your training and actually look forward to it. If you find yourself dreading the next workout, or trying to find excuses as to why you cannot train, something is wrong with your programme. It is time for a change.

PART TWO

Mountain Bike Training

4. EQUIPMENT, WARM-UP AND RECOVERY

– Appraisal of equipment required
– The warm-up
– The role of recovery

5. FLEXIBILITY

– Benefits of flexibility
– Stretching methods
– Stretching programme

6. STRENGTH TRAINING

– The theory of strength training
– Strength training tips
– Strength training programme
– Alternative strength training methods

7. FURTHER TRAINING METHODS

– Heart-rate training zones
– Anaerobic threshold training
– Interval training

- Fartlek training
- Aerobic endurance
- Plyometric training

8. PUTTING IT ALL TOGETHER

- The theory of periodisation and scheduling
- Phases making up the training year
- Year-round racing
- Training camps
- Training errors
- Being your own training coach
- Monitoring your performance

9. SPECIAL GROUPS

- Youth riders
- Junior riders
- Masters/veterans
- Female mountain bikers
- Ultra-endurance/adventure bikers
- Mountain bike tourers
- Fitness mountain bikers

10. ALTERNATIVE FORMS OF TRAINING

- The theory of cross-training
- Road cycling
- Running
- Hiking
- Swimming
- Other sports

– Muscle cramp

– Backache

– Delayed onset of muscle soreness

– Knee pain

– Nausea, dizziness and lethargy

– Masking medication

4. EQUIPMENT, WARM-UP AND RECOVERY

APPRAISAL OF EQUIPMENT REQUIRED

Part two of this book outlines how to maximise your fitness components and match them to the discipline of your choice. Because the components of fitness form the 'nuts and bolts' of any athletic training programme, the following workouts are relevant to all mountain bike categories. What does differ between disciplines is the contribution each workout makes to the overall programme. The obvious example is that every type of rider needs some degree of endurance, but it is the cross-country rider who will focus on it the most.

The workouts described in this part of the book are what you will be doing on a day-to-day basis. The application you put in here will have a snowball effect on your overall fitness level. Get it right from the start and you will reap the benefits later on. Conversely, there is the potential to go off at a tangent, blissfully unaware of any errors that are being made. Fortunately there are several types of equipment on the market that will enable you to keep a tight rein on your training, and ensure that you are doing exactly what you are supposed to be doing. Listed below are several essential items of equipment that serious mountain bike racers should have in their fitness toolbox in order to maximise training efficiency.

Heart-rate Monitor

Intensity of effort is probably the single most important factor in your mountain bike training, yet it is the most difficult to gauge subjectively. The intensity at which your heart is working ultimately determines which aspect of your fitness you develop. With the advent of the heart-rate monitor in the early 1980s, mountain bike training has taken on a more scientific approach and has never looked back.

In its basic form, a heart-rate monitor is a two-part device: a transmitter belt that sits just below your chest; and a watch-style receiver. The transmitter picks up the electrical impulses that accompany your heartbeat and sends this information wirelessly to the receiver, which displays the heart rate numerically. A heart-rate monitor can be viewed as being similar to a rev counter in a car. Just as a rev counter informs you how hard the engine is working, a heart-rate monitor tells you how hard you are working, thus removing any subjectivity.

Once the preserve of the sponsored rider, heart-rate monitors are now more accessible to the private racer. This is due mainly to the dramatic drop in cost. There are many types of heart-rate monitor on the market today, with manufacturers bringing out new models all of the time. The basic heart-rate monitors that have the sole function of representing your heart rate are adequate for your training and can easily be attached to your handlebar by fastening it to a small section of pipe insulation. These models are within the budget of most riders (£50 to £60). However, as more features are added, the cost rises quite considerably. Mid-range features include limit settings, timers, and memory recall. At the top end of the range are computer-compatible heart-rate monitors which allow you to download all your training data via an interface and save it as a file on your computer for analysis at a later stage. In addition, manufacturers such as Polar produce cycle specific heart-rate monitors which include all the functions of a heart-rate monitor plus those of a cycle computer, with added options such as cadence and altitude.

Table 3: Summary of Heart-rate Monitor Functions

FUNCTION	DESCRIPTION
HEART RATE	This tells you how hard your heart is working. Good quality training can be performed with just this information.
AVERAGE HEART RATE	During a mountain bike race, for example, your heart rate will fluctuate widely. It will soar on the climbs but will drop when you are coasting. It can often be difficult to ascertain what the average intensity of the ride was. Some heart-rate monitors have the facility to compute the average heart rate.
TRAINING ZONES	This allows you to set the limits of your training zone. If your exercise intensity falls outside your target zone, a warning alarm will sound or the display will blink.
MEMORY	This allows for heart-rate information to be stored and viewed at a later date. It is often difficult to keep an eye on your heart-rate monitor whilst navigating difficult terrain. This function allows you to recall the information for later analysis.
CALORIE COUNTER	Calculates how many calories you have used during the exercise. A good function if you are concerned about weight control.

CYCLE FUNCTIONS	Some models incorporate the usual cycle computer functions into the heart-rate monitor. They are usually supplied with a handlebar mounting system which enables easy viewing and operation whilst you are on the move.
MULTI-LINE DISPLAY	This allows you to view several displays at once. It is essential if you are performing intervals or are involved in a timed event such as a Polaris or Trailquest where it is important to know the elapsed time as well as your heart rate.
WATCH FUNCTIONS	Enables you to use your heart-rate monitor as an everyday watch.
PC COMPATIBILITY	This is the function that really hikes up the price. It enables you to download the information to your PC and monitor your progress over time. A great function if you can afford it, but is really only necessary for the professional rider or coach.

THE ROLE OF THE HEART-RATE MONITOR The role of the heart-rate monitor is to supplement your training and supply you with additional information which can help you structure your training for maximum effect. It is therefore only a training tool and not a dictator. Many riders often become a slave to their heart-rate monitors and train religiously according to prescribed heart-rate training zones. However this is not always the best approach. Sometimes you may need a rest when your heart rate indicates that you don't, or vice versa.

Heart-rate training tends to split the competitive mountain bike fraternity in two: those who favour it and those who don't. What does become apparent, though, is that the higher you go in terms of level of competition, the more the riders use heart-rate monitors as part of their training. Yes, it may detract from the freedom of mountain biking, but it also keeps a tight rein on your training and can help direct it towards your goals.

CALCULATING MAXIMUM AND MINIMUM HEART RATE In subsequent chapters we shall apply heart-rate training zones to practical workouts. This allows you to tailor your training to suit your own physiology. In order to do this you will need to find out your maximum (Hr max) and minimum (Hr min) heart rates.

The best way to determine your maximum heart rate is by performing a ramped maximal test in a sports science laboratory under medical supervision.

By its very nature the test is maximal and places a lot of strain on the body. It is possible to perform a field-test version to determine maximum heart rate, but it is imperative that there is someone there to supervise you. If you are in any doubt about your ability to exercise maximally you should consult your doctor prior to attempting the test.

For this test you will need a long hill (about 5 km) that will allow you to ride up it for about 5 minutes. With your heart rate monitor on, attack the hill at race speed. Maintain this pace until you are about 1.5 km from the top and then sprint maximally to the finish. You should attain your maximum heart rate at the top.

To calculate your minimum heart rate is a lot easier. Upon waking in the morning, put on your heart-rate monitor and lie comfortably for a few minutes. Note down your resting heart rate. It is best to do this over several days and take an average.

Once you have determined these two heart rates, you can calculate your heart-rate reserve by subtracting the Hr min from the Hr max. You can then use this figure to determine training intensities (which is discussed at length in chapter nine).

THE HEART-RATE MONITOR AND MOUNTAIN BIKING Modern scientific training methods require athletes to exercise in prescribed training zones. These training zones are depicted not by speed but by how hard the heart is working. For example, if a mountain biker is riding uphill, the speed of the rider is reduced whereas their heart rate is increased. Conversely, going downhill their speed tends to increase while their heart rate decreases. If speed were the sole determinant of training then fitness effects would be determined by the terrain.

However, in mountain biking even the heart rate is subject to large fluctuations as a result of the course profile, riding surface and weather. This can present you with a potential problem if you are attempting to exercise in a prescribed training zone. With careful manipulation of gearing and cadence, it is possible when riding off road to maintain a heart rate that is within a few beats of the training zone. However, very specific heart-rate training should be performed on the road or on a turbo/resistance trainer.

HOW THE HEART-RATE MONITOR HELPS Specific intensities have a training effect on specific fitness components. It is therefore imperative that you work within a particular training zone, otherwise a different fitness component will be trained. Knowing your heart rate is important because exercise intensity can often be difficult to judge objectively. A lack of motivation or a stressful day at work can make exercise seem harder than it actually is.

Under these conditions it is easy to terminate a workout assuming that it has been of sufficient intensity to be of benefit, when in reality your cardiovascular system has not been taxed at all. In situations such as these, a heart-rate monitor is like having a personal trainer constantly reminding you to keep going. Conversely, working too hard can be counter productive and a heart-rate monitor can be a useful ally ensuring that you keep your easy days easy and that you are not getting carried away.

Later in this chapter we shall see how the morning heart rate and orthostatic heart rate can be used to determine whether you are fully recovered from a previous workout. The morning heart rate is also a good barometer of your well-being. If one morning your heart rate is abnormally high then this may indicate that you are about to become ill – training should therefore be delayed.

Resistance Trainer

A resistance trainer is a mechanical training device that allows you to ride indoors whilst remaining stationary. Most devices attach to the rear skewer and apply resistance to the rear wheel. How the resistance is applied varies. Some models use a fan (often referred to as a turbo trainer), others use magnets, or fluid. Nowadays, many health clubs and gymnasiums have stationary bicycle ergometers which allow for indoor training, and most of these have advanced functions such as power output, energy expenditure and heart-rate monitoring. Although these functions are of a distinct advantage, they are more than offset by the poor riding position and lack of clipless pedals. With these ergometers the riding position tends to be more upright than on a race-prepared mountain bike, whereas with resistance trainers you are riding on your own bike. Riding without clipless pedals will also interfere with maintaining the correct pedalling action (chapter twelve).

Resistance trainers make working within a prescribed heart-rate zone relatively easy and, despite being a rather monotonous way to train, they can be a valuable training tool. In addition to allowing an alternative medium for training when the weather is inclement, a resistance trainer enables you to perform accurate interval sessions without having to worry about undulating terrain or hazardous traffic situations.

As with the heart-rate monitors, the models and cost of resistance trainers differ quite considerably. The lower-priced models typically offer wind resistance which you alter by changing gear, and whilst providing adequate resistance, they can be noisy in use and often do not allow for a smooth pedal stroke. Fluid and magnetic resistance trainers are much quieter in use and most models allow the user to alter resistance by a remote lever which can be attached to the handlebars. Extra features on more expensive models include power output and cadence information. Some models are also computer compatible and enable you to simulate a race with other riders, or to ride your favourite international course. These extra features certainly go some way to alleviating the boredom traditionally associated with turbo trainer workouts.

Training Diary

An accurate training diary is an excellent source of training information. It allows you to view your training longitudinally and monitor your progress carefully over a period of time. Throughout your training year there will be times when you are required to perform fitness tests. These tests will give you a snapshot view of fitness status at that particular point in time. Fitness tests are naturally very intense and they place a lot of strain on your body. Because of this they must be used sparingly. Similarly, competing in a mountain bike race is the ultimate determinant of your fitness levels. However, racing is also physically demanding, and is limited mainly to the race season. There is therefore a large amount of time where your fitness is not checked. It is this gap that the training diary attempts to fill.

Completing a training diary on a daily basis can often be a laborious and monotonous task, but it takes less than five minutes to complete and is well worth the effort in the long run. In subsequent chapters I will detail how to design a training programme and how to fill in your training diary and ascribe workouts to specific days. In its most basic form a training diary allows you to check that you have done what you were supposed to have done. Over time you can analyse this and see if your workouts have had sufficient intensity. If there are any discrepancies then something is wrong and re-evaluation is needed. With a training diary, factors which may have otherwise gone unnoticed can easily come to light. Fluctuations in bodyweight or resting heart rate are important sources of information because they reflect your training status and well-being.

Nowadays, the majority of the computer-compatible heart-rate monitors come complete with logbook software, and update the daily entries each time a file is downloaded. The data can then be represented in graphical form and subsequently analysed. This is ideal if you are computer literate, but can be somewhat cumbersome if you are not.

WHAT TO INCLUDE The basic information you need for a training diary is as follows:

1. Morning heart-rate and orthostatic test
The protocols for both of these tests are detailed at the end of this chapter. They are crucial sources of information when it comes to assessing your fitness status.

2. Desired and actual workout

The training programmes that are given in subsequent chapters will require you to exercise in precise heart-rate zones. However, this is often easier said than done. You should log both your prescribed workout and your actual workout.

3. Weather

Most of your training will be outdoors so it is at the mercy of the weather. Your mountain bike performance will fluctuate widely if your workouts are performed in headwinds, boggy mud, or extreme temperatures. As such you should record these conditions so that you can take them into account when you review your diary at a later date.

4. Sleep pattern

Your sleep pattern and recovery status are closely related. One or two poor nights' sleep can be accommodated without cause for concern. However, if there is a prolonged period where your sleep pattern is disturbed then this may reflect a hidden problem. Poor sleep is often associated with over-training.

5. Mental comments

Both your motivation and enthusiasm play crucial roles in your workouts, especially when the intensity is raised. Ultimately it is your brain that says when you've had enough and it is time to quit a workout. Record how you are feeling and how motivated you are.

6. Physical comments

Enter any physical feelings that you think are relevant. Are you feeling run down? Do your legs feel powerful? Are there any twinges? Write them all down.

A training diary is only of any real use if it is completed on a regular basis. At the end of every workout you should enter the information immediately while it is still fresh in your mind.

ANALYSIS OF THE TRAINING DIARY It is important that you analyse your training and evaluate your mountain bike performance on a regular basis. You should glance over your daily entries and compare your prescribed training with your actual workout. If there is any discrepancy between the two, try to deduce what the cause of the disparity is. On a weekly and monthly basis you should spend some time analysing your diary so far. See if you can find any relationships between your heart rates, your bodyweight, how you are feeling, what you ate, your sleep patterns and so on. Examine your good performances and also your bad ones. Is there a pattern emerging as to why you performed this way? It now becomes easy to see what factors improve your fitness. Obviously these should then be reproduced in the future, in order to maximise your fitness. Just as

Table 4: A Typical Page from a Mountain Biker's Training Diary

DATE: Monday	DATE: 17 April

MORNING HR: [45] ORTHOSTATIC HR: [55] WEIGHT: [70 kg]

SLEEP DURATION [8 hours] WEATHER [sunny – no wind]

DESIRED WORKOUT: 1 hour endurance ride @ ATI followed by 30 mins flexibility work.

ACTUAL WORKOUT: 1 hour endurance ride, but some of it slightly below ATI threshold. Completed all 30 mins of flexibility work.

HEART-RATE ZONE: TIME IN: [50 mins] TIME ABOVE: [2 mins] TIME BELOW: [8 mins]

PHYSICAL COMMENTS: Felt pretty strong today, although legs were a little heavy from yesterday. Couldn't stay in training zone.

MENTAL COMMENTS: No problems here, I was raring to go!

OTHER COMMENTS: Ate a Powerbar 30 mins before the endurance ride and my energy levels were up for the whole ride.

important, though, are the things that reduce your performance. Once you know what they are, you can avoid them.

THE WARM-UP

This is the procedure a rider performs prior to a competition or training in order to prepare, both physically and mentally, for the upcoming exercise. The aim of a warm-up is to reach an optimal body core and muscle temperature, which subsequently makes the body more efficient during exercise. The physical warming up of the muscles, tendons and ligaments makes them more elastic and less susceptible to strains and injury. Scientific studies have shown that far greater forces are required to tear a 'warmed-up' muscle compared to its cold counterpart. The increase in temperature also provides the optimal chemical environment within the muscles; increases the metabolic rate; and facilitates oxygen and fuel transportation to the working muscles. In other words, a warm-up primes your body's systems and gets them ready for exercise.

Many riders report feeling more 'psyched up' for a race after they have performed a warm-up. It gets them into the correct frame of mind prior to the race. It also improves their confidence because they feel that they can go 'all-out' without the fear of causing an injury.

Mountain Biking and the Warm-up

Start your warm-up with some general exercises for the whole body. Following a light jog, you should perform a routine of bodyweight exercises which move your muscles and joints through their full range of motion. Typical exercises include bodyweight squats, jogging on the spot, neck rolls and shoulder circles. Perform these until you break into a light sweat.

The emphasis of your warm-up should now focus on the specific muscles and joints that you will be using more intensely later on. Spin easy on your bike and slowly move up through the gears until you feel sufficiently warmed-up. It is important that you do not get fatigued during your warm-up and deplete your glycogen stores. Remember you are only *preparing* your body for exercise. You should now perform a series of stretches, paying particular emphasis to the muscles that you are going to be using. For information about stretching, see chapter five.

The benefits of a warm-up are transient and are only most effective for a couple of minutes afterwards. There is a gradual loss of the effects of a warm-up during inactivity and this is known as the warm-up decrement. This presents a problem for the mountain bike racer. Typically at a race it is advantageous to be at the front at the start in order to get the best racing line; however, as the best positions are taken early, there usually involves a waiting period of inactivity. A trade-off exists between the benefits of a good start position and those of a warm-up. In this situation it is best to leave it until the last possible moment before you line up. Wear some warm clothes and have someone collect them just prior to the start.

THE ROLE OF RECOVERY

Recovery is the name given to the physiological processes that occur in your body following training in order to restore it to its pre-exercise condition. The time your body takes to do this is called the recovery period. In order to optimise the effect of your mountain bike training, you must ensure that you are fully recovered between workouts and that you do not begin a subsequent training bout until you are fully recovered.

Clearly, the length of your recovery period can be a severe limiting factor to your training volume and ultimately your mountain bike fitness. For example, if rider A has a recovery period of 24 hours and rider B has a recovery period of 48 hours, rider A can perform a greater number of intense workouts in a given time period compared to rider B. It is therefore a distinct advantage to be able to facilitate your recovery period and there are a number of ways that you can achieve this.

Recovery following a training ride can actually be enhanced before and during the ride as well as after it. A thorough warm-up before training or competition reduces the trauma associated with exercise and so acts as a form of damage limitation with regard to post-exercise recovery. The replacement of spent carbohydrates during exercise is a potent factor in reducing the recovery period. Consume between half a litre and one litre of a 15 per cent carbohydrate drink every hour during your ride, as this aids the recovery of the energy production system (see chapter fifteen). Making sure that your body is fully hydrated throughout the exercise bout is of paramount importance, not only to performance, but also to ensuring full recovery.

It has been shown that during the recovery period muscle glycogen and phosphagen stores are replenished and the by-products of exercise – such as lactic acid and other metabolites – are removed. It is also during the recovery period that adaptation and protein replacement occur and you become fitter. As a result it is good practice to consume further carbohydrates following exercise so as to maximise glycogen storage.

There are two main physical procedures employed to enhance the recovery process, namely passive and active recovery. As the name suggests passive recovery involves doing nothing. Here the rider rests (typically lying down) with the assumption that recovery will be enhanced by reducing the energy demand of the body. This has only been shown to be effective for sub-maximal exercise, and as such is not really applicable to mountain bikers, despite it often being their first choice of recovery! Instead, active recovery has been found to be of greater benefit.

Active recovery, or cooling down or tapering off as it is otherwise known, involves light to moderate cycling following a vigorous ride. It is believed that active rest, in addition to aiding recovery, reduces the risk of injury and muscle soreness. For mountain bikers, active rest should involve cycling at an easy intensity for at least 30 minutes. Training status can greatly influence the rate of recovery. The fitter you are the shorter your recovery period will become. Taking a hot bath, shower or sauna after completion of a hard workout aids relaxation and recovery, as does ultrasound and massage. And of course good dietary practice is essential, for your body must have all the materials to hand if it is to rebuild itself.

Massage

In an ideal world you would receive a massage both before and after every bike ride from a qualified massage therapist. Lamentably, this tends to be the preserve only of the sponsored professional rider. Fortunately, however, it is possible to glean many of the benefits from self-massage. The benefits of massage for the mountain biker are many. Massaging a muscle, or group of muscles, helps to increase their temperature and improve the blood circulation to the area. This is ideal before a strenuous workout in order to prepare the muscle for the forthcoming exercise. It is also important after an intense ride because the improved circulation coupled with the mechanical action of massaging helps to remove metabolic by-products, such as lactic acid, from the muscles. Massaging also causes muscles to become more relaxed and is therefore a relevant precursor to stretching. It can also help to relieve painful muscle cramps – and of course it feels good!

SELF MASSAGE Self-massage is really very easy. All you have to do is rub and knead your muscles so that they relax. Relaxation of your muscles is the key. Don't press so hard that your muscles tense up as a result. The process is made a whole lot easier if you use massage oil or talc. If you have particularly hairy legs you may find the process painful because your hairs will get pulled as a result of the massaging action. If this is the case, you may want to consider shaving your legs, which is the reason why the professional mountain bikers do.

Below is a self-help massage guide to get you started. I've targeted the key muscles involved in mountain biking, though I'm sure there will be other muscles that will be aching after a hard day in the saddle. Don't be afraid to apply the principles to those ones as well – just remember not to massage any muscle that is injured.

Table 5: Self-massage Summary

MUSCLE	MASSAGE PROCEDURE
Soleus and gastrocnemius (calves)	These are a great muscles to massage. You should massage each calf with both hands, kneading deep into the muscle with your thumbs. You should start at the base of the calves and work up, as this helps remove any toxins.
Quadriceps (the large muscle on the front of the upper thigh)	After a tough mountain bike ride, the quadriceps are typically heavily fatigued and full of the by-products of exercise. You should massage the quadriceps with your fingers, thumbs and palms. Alternate deep kneading actions with lighter strokes. Again, you should work from the bottom upwards.

Hamstrings (the large muscle on the back of the upper thigh)	The hamstring muscles are notoriously prone to cramping. A good post-ride massage will help prevent this. Alternate deep kneading actions with lighter strokes. Again, you should work from the bottom upwards.
Glutes (the muscles of your backside)	Work the entire area with your fingers and thumbs. Where it is particularly fleshy, knead deeply, but avoid pressing too hard near bony areas (which could result in trapped nerves).

Recovery Tests

Having a good recovery period is often referred to as having 'good physiology' and is also an excellent indicator of your fitness and health status. Below are several tests that you can perform to assess the progress of your recovery ability. Remember to make sure that the conditions are similar each time you test.

RECOVERY RATE FIELD TEST 1

PURPOSE: This test monitors your ability to recover following an intense bout of exercise.

PROCEDURE: Find a quiet stretch of road with a long hill.

Ride as fast as possible up the hill (for no more than 2 minutes), keeping your pace as consistent as possible.

Record your time and your final heart rate (using a heart-rate monitor).

Rest for 3 minutes and then record your recovery heart rate.

Subtract your recovery heart rate from your exercise heart rate and note down the 'difference' figure.

Perform this test at regular intervals (about a month apart) and compare results. A greater 'difference' figure (or a faster time for the same figure) indicates an improved rate of recovery.

TESTING TIP: Use the same location, same start and finish points, comparable weather, and ensure that you are fully recovered beforehand.

RECOVERY RATE FIELD TEST 2

PURPOSE: This test monitors your ability to recover in between a series of repeated exercise bouts.

PROCEDURE: On a flat section of open ground, place two markers 60 m apart.

Approach the first marker and sprint maximally to the next one. Have an assistant record your time.

Recover for 20 seconds by cycling at an easy pace.

Repeat the above procedure until you have completed eight sprints.

You can now convert your times into a fatigue index which can be used to assess your ability to recover between sprints. In theory, if all your sprints are the same then you have fully recovered during each rest period. If you fail to recover fully then you should notice an increase in sprint time as the test progresses. Use the following equation to calculate your fatigue index:

$$\frac{(T7 + T8)}{2} - \frac{(T1 + T2)}{2} = D$$

$$\text{Fatigue Index (\%)} = \frac{D}{(T1 + T2)/2} \times 100$$

A low Fatigue Index score indicates a good ability to recover.

0% = Full recovery

100% = Fully fatigued

TESTING TIP: In order to get meaningful and accurate results, don't pace yourself during this test; go maximally on every sprint.

ORTHOSTATIC HEART-RATE TEST

PURPOSE: The orthostatic (standing) test is a simple procedure for monitoring recovery status. It is based on changes in heart-rate values caused by standing erect following a period of being supine (lying down face-up).

PROCEDURE: Lie supine and rest for 15 minutes.

Record your heart rate.

Stand up and, after 15 seconds, record your heart rate again.

Subtract the supine heart-rate value from the standing heart-rate value.

The typical figure for this value for a fully recovered individual is below 15 beats per minute. If it is greater than 20 then you have not fully recovered from your training.

TESTING TIP: This information is only relevant if you do it every day, so get into the habit of performing this test every morning.

MORNING HEART-RATE TEST

Every morning, shortly after waking, take a heart-rate reading. Over a period of time you should be able to establish a typical waking heart rate. As you become fitter this value should drop. However, a rise in morning heart rate usually signifies incomplete recovery.

SUBJECTIVE RECOVERY TEST

After you have been following a training schedule for an extended period of time you will gain experience from the heart-rate monitor and associated feelings and be able to 'read', as well as monitor, your body. Typical feelings of complete recovery include a strong desire to train, good sleeping pattern, positive attitude, and a feeling of well-being and good health.

5. FLEXIBILITY

BENEFITS OF FLEXIBILITY

Flexibility is perhaps the most underestimated and undervalued component of mountain bike fitness. You may be forgiven for thinking that its role in mountain biking is limited, especially if you compare it to other sports such as gymnastics where the need for flexibility is more obvious. However, scratch beneath the surface and it soon becomes apparent that flexibility plays a major part in your mountain biking fitness, and it can have a major influence on the longevity of your racing career.

When implemented correctly, a stretching programme can offer many benefits to the mountain biker which include:

ENHANCED PHYSICAL FITNESS As we have already discussed in chapter one, flexibility is an integral component of your physical fitness. If flexibility is your weak link, an improvement in this area will complete your fitness jigsaw and make you a more rounded athlete.

IMPROVEMENT IN POSTURE Poor posture can often be traced to muscular imbalance and inferior flexibility. This is especially rife in sports such as mountain biking where the posture of the rider is hunched up and the limbs are rarely stretched. An improvement in your flexibility will enable your posture to return to normal and give you the added benefit of avoiding the auxiliary problems associated with chronic joint misalignment.

REDUCED MUSCLE TENSION AND IMPROVED PERFORMANCE Tight, inflexible muscles will lead to tension that will be both uncomfortable and unhealthy. An improvement in your flexibility will result in unrestricted muscles and less tension. This will also improve your mountain bike efficiency, because your working muscles will have to overcome less resistance and therefore use less energy.

REDUCED MUSCLE SORENESS Research indicates that if a stretching programme is performed after rigorous exercise it will help facilitate recovery and alleviate delayed muscle soreness. This will mean that you can train sooner and, as a result, you will get fitter quicker.

REDUCED RISK OF INJURY TO JOINTS, MUSCLES, TENDONS AND LIGAMENTS Flexibility training will increase the range of motion at your joints. If your joints are suddenly moved in an unfamiliar action, such as during a crash, then the likelihood of walking away without an injury will be greater if you are flexible.

PREPARATION OF THE MUSCLES FOR THE IMPENDING EXERCISE Because of the responses highlighted above, performing stretching exercises prior to exercising will help increase the readiness of your muscles and improve their response to exercise. In a race scenario this means you will be ready from the very start – not after a few minutes once they have been loosened.

INCREASED MENTAL AND PHYSICAL RELAXATION The act of stretching not only physically slackens your muscles, but, if performed correctly, can also lead to a state of mental relaxation.

ENHANCED DEVELOPMENT OF BODY AWARENESS Feeling the stretching and tension in your muscles leads to an improved neuro-muscular knowledge which in turn increases your kinaesthetic awareness.

A REDUCTION IN THE TENDENCY OF MUSCLES TO SHORTEN AND TIGHTEN FOLLOWING TRAINING When you are mountain biking, there is very little time during the pedalling action when your legs are straight. They are denied the opportunity fully to extend or flex, and because of this the range of motion at the knee is limited. As a result the muscles on the back of your thigh (the hamstrings) are never stretched. This condition can lead to a gradual shortening of the muscle and consequent injury unless an appropriate stretching programme is implemented.

ENJOYMENT Performing stretching exercises feels good.

Flexibility, like any other component of physical fitness, is subject to the principles of training, and if performed correctly it can drastically increase your performance. However, if performed erroneously, stretching may hinder your mountain bike progress. The most common mistakes include:

INAPPROPRIATE WARM-UP Muscles, joints and connective tissue are more susceptible to injuries and tears if they are cold. Subjecting your body to a flexibility workout is asking for trouble if you haven't adequately warmed up. It follows, therefore, that it is counterproductive to use stretching solely as your warm-up. In order to reduce the likelihood of muscle, tendon and ligament impairment, you should only include your stretching regimen after your general warm-up, when your muscles are warmer and more pliable.

INADEQUATE REST BETWEEN WORKOUTS In order for your muscles and connective tissue to adapt to the stretches and fully supercompensate, you are going to have to give them time. If you are a beginner, or are new to flexibility training, you should avoid performing rigorous stretching protocols on consecutive days.

OVER-STRETCHING We all have the potential to improve significantly our flexibility; but only if we are patient. Like all aspects of our fitness, the whole process takes time and cannot be rushed. Many beginners want immediate gratification and will endeavour to reach further, even if it hurts. Over-stretching your muscles and connective tissue is obviously dangerous and will inevitably lead to injury.

PERFORMING THE STRETCHES INCORRECTLY Incorrect technique when stretching can often be worse than performing no flexibility work at all. Because you are placing your muscles, joints and connective tissue under considerable strain, it is imperative that you use only safe exercises and adhere to strict form.

STRETCHING METHODS

There are several types of stretching methods available for you to use, the predominant ones being: static; ballistic; and proprioceptive neuro-muscular facilitation (PNF). Ballistic stretching involves dynamic 'bouncing' in order to increase the range of motion at a joint. If it is practised by an unsupervised novice it can rapidly lead to injury. PNF stretching is a more complicated form of stretching and can also be dangerous if performed by the unskilled. We will focus solely on static stretching, as this method is effective, relatively safe, can be done on your own with minimal equipment, and is applicable to mountain biking.

Before we go any further it is important that you have an understanding of the physiology of a muscle and what happens to it when it is stretched. Deep within a skeletal muscle there are special receptors known as muscle spindles. These are safety mechanisms that are sensitive to stretch. If a muscle is elongated rapidly, or over-stretched, the muscle spindle counteracts this potentially harmful action by initiating a reflex message via the spinal cord which causes the muscle to contract. This is known as a stretch reflex and is a preventative measure to stop the muscle from tearing. This stretch reflex lasts for about ten seconds, and then if no harm has been done it switches off. With the stretch reflex turned off, it is now possible to stretch a little further until the stretch reflex is initiated once again. To profit from this and reap the maximum effect, you should hold your stretches for at least 30 seconds.

In accordance with the specificity principle, each flexibility exercise you perform should only stretch the muscles that you are attempting to stretch. Isolating the individual muscles means that you only have to overcome the resistance of the antagonist (opposing) muscle alone. This offers a more sensitive gauge of the intensity of the stretch and ultimately gives you more control over the exercise thus minimising the risk of injury.

The potential risk of injury from performing a particular stretch must be taken into consideration from a personal perspective. A mild amount of discomfort is often associated with stretching, but if you experience any pain before, during, or after stretching you must stop immediately and identify the cause (which will probably be one of the four common mistakes mentioned earlier). Although a particular stretch may be highly regarded as being effective in enhancing flexibility, you must always be aware that it may not complement your biomechanics or injury history. If this is the case then omit the troublesome exercise from your programme and substitute it with another more appropriate one. There are many excellent books on the market dedicated to sports injuries, rehabilitation and stretching, containing a plethora of exercises for you to choose from.

The following stretching programme is designed to increase your flexibility and complement your mountain biking. After having performed the exercises you should not feel sore. If you do then you have over-stretched and caused microscopic trauma to the muscle. To avoid over-stretching, you should perform the exercise until you are able to feel the tension in the muscle, but no more. Exhale as you move into the stretch, hold the position for 30 seconds breathing rhythmically, then move out of the stretch with as much care as you went in to it. You should aim to perform as many sets of the stretch as it takes in order to reach your maximum range of motion (usually four). Perform the stretches in the order they are given. It is important to note that if you are stretching prior to a ride, rather than to increase flexibility per se, you should not work the muscles to the point of fatigue. Save your energy for your riding.

STRETCHING PROGRAMME

NECK ROLLS

PURPOSE: During mountain biking the jarring effect of the trail combined with the bracing of the shoulder muscles can lead to tension in the neck area. The following stretch targets the entire neck and relieves muscular tension.

PROCEDURE: In a standing position, gently and slowly roll your neck through its full range of motion. Do this ten times in each direction.

STRETCHING TIP: As you roll your neck through its full range of motion, there will be tight spots where the neck muscles will feel taut. When you encounter one of these, stop and hold the stretch for several seconds before continuing.

Neck rolls

NECK SIDE STRETCH

PURPOSE: This is an excellent stretch for releasing neck and shoulder tension.

PROCEDURE: Stand upright, looking straight ahead with your hands clasped behind your back.

Now lower your right ear to your right shoulder, whilst simultaneously pulling your left arm downwards with your right hand.

STRETCHING TIP: Hold the stretch, relax and then repeat with the other side.

Neck side stretch

ARM AND SHOULDER STRETCH

PURPOSE: This stretch promotes mobility in the shoulder area.

PROCEDURE: Stand upright with your hands clasped behind your lower back.

Keeping your arms straight, lift your arms behind you in a backwards arch. You should feel the stretch in your shoulders, across your chest and in your arms.

Hold the stretch and relax.

STRETCHING TIP: To maximise this stretch, push your chest out and keep your chin tucked in.

Arm and shoulder stretch

OVERHEAD ARM AND SHOULDER STRETCH

PURPOSE: This exercise also increases shoulder mobility, but also stretches the back of the upper arm (the triceps).

PROCEDURE: Stand upright and lift your left arm straight up.

Bend your left elbow, and with your right hand gently pull your left elbow behind your head.

Hold the stretch and relax, then repeat with the other arm.

STRETCHING TIP: You may find that you have one shoulder that is more flexible than the other. If this is so spend a little more time on your weak shoulder and bring it up to par.

Overhead arm and shoulder

FOREARM STRETCH

PURPOSE: Trail buzz and downhill biking fatigue the forearm muscles very quickly. This exercise is a great way to improve the flexibility of your forearm muscles and facilitate their recovery.

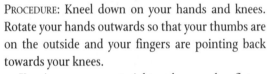

PROCEDURE: Kneel down on your hands and knees. Rotate your hands outwards so that your thumbs are on the outside and your fingers are pointing back towards your knees.

Keeping your arms straight and your palms flat on the floor, slowly lean back until you can feel a comfortable stretch in your forearm muscles.

Hold the stretch and relax.

Forearm stretch

STRETCHING TIPS: Make sure you keep the heel of your hand on the floor at all times.

Most mountain bikers have relatively tight forearms, so start off gradually and don't force the stretch.

SIDE STRETCH

PURPOSE: This exercise targets the muscles on the side of your torso (the obliques) and is a great stretch to do after a long day in the saddle.

PROCEDURE: Stand upright with your feet about shoulder-width apart.

Raise your left hand over your head and place your right hand on the outside of your right thigh.

Slowly and carefully bend to your right. Let your right hand slide down your right thigh. You can use your right hand for support if you need it. You should feel a comfortable stretch along the left side of your torso.

Hold the stretch and carefully and deliberately return to the start position.

Repeat with the other side.

STRETCHING TIPS: Make sure that you only bend to the side. Do not lean forwards or backwards.

Avoid the temptation to hold your breath when you are performing this stretch. Make a conscious effort to breathe normally.

In the beginning, only hold the stretch for ten seconds. As you become more comfortable with the exercise, gradually increase the time that you spend in the stretch until you can do it for 30 seconds.

Side stretch

KNEELING LOWER BACK STRETCH

PURPOSE: This is an excellent exercise to increase the range of motion in your vertebrae and to loosen any knotted or tight muscles in your back.

PROCEDURE: Kneel down on your hands and knees. Then, without moving your arms or legs, simultaneously lower your head whilst arching your back upwards. Hold the stretch and relax.

Then perform the reverse of the above. Raise your head whilst lowering your spine to form a hollow. Hold the stretch and relax.

STRETCHING TIPS: Make the movements slow and deliberate.

Avoid the temptation to hold your breath when you are performing this stretch. Make a conscious effort to breathe normally.

Kneeling lower back stretch

ABDOMINALS/LOWER BACK STRETCH

PURPOSE: This stretching exercise increases the range of motion in your vertebrae and also stretches your abdominal muscles. It is an excellent stretch to perform after you have done a set of sit-ups.

PROCEDURE: Lie on your front, as if you are about to perform a press-up. Then, without moving your hands or feet, straighten your arms and arch your back.

Look upwards, so that your whole spine hyper-extends and you can feel a comfortable stretch in your abdominals.

Hold the stretch and relax.

STRETCHING TIP: Avoid the temptation to hold your breath when you are performing this stretch. Make a conscious effort to breathe normally.

Abdominals/lower back
stretch

SEATED TWIST STRETCH

PURPOSE: This exercise targets your upper and lower back, as well as your hip area. It is an excellent stretch to perform after a long day in the saddle.

PROCEDURE: Sit down with both legs extended in front of you. Then bend your left leg and cross it over your right, so that the heel of your left foot is touching the outside of your right knee.

With your left hand resting behind you for support, rotate your torso towards your bent knee and place your right elbow on the outside of your left knee.

Seated twist stretch

Turn your head over your left shoulder and look behind you. At the same time apply controlled pressure to your left knee with your right elbow.

Hold the stretch and relax, then repeat with the other side.

STRETCHING TIPS: Throughout the stretch, ensure that your hips do not move.

Avoid the temptation to hold your breath when you are performing this stretch. Make a conscious effort to breathe normally.

GROIN STRETCH

PURPOSE: This is a good exercise to improve the flexibility in your hip and groin area.

PROCEDURE: Sit down with the soles of your feet together, then bring them as close to

your groin as possible. Hold your ankles and bend forward slightly at the hips whilst maintaining a straight back. Hold this stretch for a few seconds.

Now gently press down on your knees with your elbows until you feel a good stretch in your groin.

Groin stretch

Hold the stretch and relax.

STRETCHING TIPS: Only bend slightly forward at the hips. Do not round your back.

Only after you have settled into the first part of the stretch, and you are stable, should you proceed with stretching the groin area.

STANDING CALF STRETCH

PURPOSE: During a mountain bike ride your calves are continually worked. They are involved in every pedal stroke and have to support your bodyweight when you stand up on your pedals and coast. Flexible calf muscles will result in a more ergonomic pedal stroke and reduce the likelihood of the muscles cramping.

PROCEDURE: Stand in front of a wall and step forward with your left foot. Assume a position as if you were attempting to push the wall over and make sure that both of your feet are pointing straight ahead.

Keeping your feet parallel and your heels on the ground, slowly bend your left knee and move your hips forward. Throughout the stretch, you should keep your right leg straight and your lower back flat. You should feel a stretch in your right calf muscle.

Standing calf stretch

Hold the stretch and relax, then repeat with the other leg.

STRETCHING TIP: Keep your heels on the floor throughout the stretch.

HAMSTRING STRETCH

PURPOSE: Mountain bikers notoriously have tight hamstrings. This is because the hamstring muscle is rarely stretched during the cycling action. Once you are off the bike, tight hamstrings can exert an uneven pull on your pelvis and cause postural problems. They are often the cause of lower back pain.

PROCEDURE: Sit down with both legs extended in front of you and place the sole of your right foot against the inside of your left thigh.

Without bending your left leg, lean forward at the hips and try to hold your left ankle.

Hold the stretch and relax, then repeat with the other side.

Hamstring stretch

STRETCHING TIPS: Do not dip your head during the stretch. Look at the foot of your outstretched leg.

Keep the foot of your outstretched leg pointing straight upwards.

Ensure that the quadriceps muscles of your outstretched leg are relaxed.

QUADRICEPS STRETCH

PURPOSE: This is a good exercise for stretching the large muscle group on the front of your thigh (the quadriceps). It is a particularly good exercise for bringing a bit of life back into tired legs.

PROCEDURE: Stand upright on your right leg and bring your left heel to your buttock. Take hold of your left foot with your left hand.

With your left knee pointing towards the floor, gently pull your left foot backwards until you feel a stretch in your frontal thigh.

Hold the stretch and relax, then repeat with the other leg.

STRETCHING TIPS: If you have problems balancing whilst holding this stretch, hold on to something for support, although with practice you should be able to do it free-standing.

Quadriceps stretch

This stretch can also be performed on the floor. Lying face down, reach behind you with your left hand and hold onto your left foot. Then continue with the above procedure.

As we have discussed in chapter four, stretching should not only be a workout in its own right, but it should also be part of the cooling down process because it helps to reduce muscle fatigue and soreness. Furthermore, if you are still sore or tight the day after an intense ride, perform a light stretching routine to help reduce the lingering tenderness and tautness.

Stretching on the Bike

There are times whilst you are on your mountain bike when it may be advantageous to perform some stretches. If you are involved in an ultra-endurance event, or a touring expedition, you can relieve your tired muscles and inject a bit of life back into them with a few simple stretches. If you are in a race you may need to stretch a muscle to prevent it from cramping. The following simple stretches can be performed when you are on the move. It stands to reason that these exercises should only be performed on easy terrain, where you can see well ahead, and where you are not going to cause any harm either to yourself or to another rider.

BACK/NECK STRETCH

PURPOSE: This stretch can be used to alleviate tense shoulder and back muscles. You can also use it to help relieve tired muscles in your neck that have become fatigued as a result of maintaining an upright head position so that you can look forwards and keep an eye on the terrain.

PROCEDURE: At a safe section of terrain, sit down and coast.

Arch your back and allow your chin touch to your chest. Stretch this position as far as possible.

Back/neck stretch

Hold this stretch momentarily, then resume your normal riding position.

STRETCHING TIP: If the terrain permits, repeat the above procedure as many times as is necessary.

QUADRICEPS STRETCH

PURPOSE: This is an excellent way of refreshing your quadriceps muscles during a hard ride or race. In order to perform this stretch you need a good sense of balance and co-ordination. It is therefore wise to practise this stretch on your training rides rather than for the first time in a race.

PROCEDURE: At a safe section of terrain, sit down and coast.

Shift your bodyweight over your saddle and unclip your fatigued leg. Bring your right foot up to your buttocks and hold onto it with your right hand.

Quadriceps stretch

Hold the stretch for as long as possible, then return your foot to the pedal.

STRETCHING TIP: If terrain permits, repeat with the other leg if necessary.

LOWER BACK STRETCH

PURPOSE: It is very common in mountain bike racing for the lower back to be a source of pain and great discomfort. If you find yourself suffering from lower back fatigue, the following stretch will give you a bit of respite from it.

PROCEDURE: At a safe section of terrain, coast. Then shift your body forwards and downwards as if you are about to sit on the top tube just behind your stem.

Hover above the top tube without actually sitting on it.

Simultaneously stick your chest out and form a hollow in your lower back.

Return to your normal riding position.

STRETCHING TIP: Repeat this procedure as many times as is necessary.

Lower back stretch

CALF STRETCH

PURPOSE: After prolonged sections of terrain where you have had to remain out of the saddle – such as a particularly fearsome downhill section – your calves may

become fatigued and feel as if they are on fire. To relieve this sensation and to avoid cramp try the following stretch.

PROCEDURE: At a safe section of terrain, coast. Then stand out of the saddle with the cranks horizontal.

With only a slight bend in your legs, slowly lower your heels so that they are below the pedal axles. You should feel the stretch in your calf muscles.

Calf stretch

STRETCHING TIP: The stretch should be most intense in the rear leg, so repeat the procedure having first altered the cranks 180°.

6. STRENGTH TRAINING

THE THEORY OF STRENGTH TRAINING

Strength training is a very important, yet often overlooked, aspect of mountain bike fitness training. The very nature of mountain biking places a great demand on the muscles of the body, especially those in the limbs and lower back as they are forced to absorb the shock of the undulating terrain, the drop-offs and the inevitable crashes. There may also be times in your racing career when you are forced to carry your bike for various sections of the course. Lifting a lightweight mountain bike may not sound too bad right now, but when you're on your last lap and your bike is caked in mud it will feel like an old 30-pound clunker. It is therefore advantageous for you to develop a sound muscular infrastructure so that you can accommodate the physical beatings that mountain bike racing throws at you. Weak auxiliary muscles also play a critical role in the loss of form when a rider is fatigued. This is evident at races across all the disciplines of mountain biking. Cross-country riders completing their final lap, or downhill competitors on the last stretch of the course, often display poor form because their muscles are fatigued and won't respond. This inevitably leads to a subsequent drop in riding efficiency, which could have been avoided if strengthening exercises had been included in their training programme.

You should incorporate strength training into your programme, not to develop muscle hypertrophy per se, but for the rather less cosmetic role of facilitating muscular power and strength. In addition to these prized components, strengthening exercises also improve all-round body conditioning by bringing under-developed muscles up to par. Unfortunately, mountain biking on its own promotes muscular imbalance. Certain muscles, such as the quadriceps (the large muscles on the front of your thigh), are continually used and as a result they adapt by becoming bigger and stronger. Other muscles, such as the hamstrings (the muscles on the back of your thigh), are stressed less and so do not develop at the same rate. If left unchecked, this can create an uneven pull on the knee joint and can eventually lead to a chronic injury. It is therefore important to perform strengthening exercises for the hamstrings in order to avoid potential knee problems. Similarly, mountain biking stresses the lower back muscles more than it stresses the abdominal muscles. This predicament causes an uneven pull on the spine and can lead to postural deficiencies. Again it is important to perform strengthening exercises for the weaker muscles in order to restore correct muscle balance.

As good as it is, strength work should only supplement your training and not detract from it. By its very nature, strength training is an intense activity and it can cause you serious damage if you are lifting weights with poor technique. It is therefore imperative that you maintain the correct lifting procedure at all times. An injured body means time out of the saddle, which in turn means a subsequent reduction in your mountain bike fitness due to a detraining effect. The key here is to leave your ego behind when you visit the gym and lift conservatively. Remember you are a mountain biker, not a body builder.

You should perform two strength workouts per week, with each one lasting no longer than 60 minutes. As with all of your training, you should divide your strength work up into distinct phases (see chapter eight) with each phase focusing on a particular aspect of your strength. Your first strength phase is a general conditioning programme which should run in conjunction with your foundation phase and last for between 10 to 15 weeks. During this phase you should concentrate on developing all-round, well-balanced strength. Your aim during this period should be to develop a flawless strength base upon which you can build during the following phases.

The second stage is a power and strength programme which should supplement your preparation phases (P1 and P2 phases; see chapter eight) and should last for approximately 15 weeks. It is during this period that you will be lifting your heaviest weights. The third and final phase is muscular endurance based and should coincide with your race season.

STRENGTH TRAINING TIPS

No matter what training phase you are in, there are several guidelines to which you should constantly adhere:

1. Prior to every strength training session you should perform a thorough warm-up. If you are scheduled to lift heavy weights, as in the power and strength programme, it is advisable to increase the length of the warm-up accordingly. Following the warm-up you should then perform a full body-stretching routine, paying particular attention to the muscles that you are going to exercise.
2. Perform all of the strength exercises in a slow, controlled manner. Ensure that you always concentrate on strict form and do not let your execution of the

exercise become sloppy in order to lift heavy weights. Concentrate and focus on the muscle, or muscles, you are exercising.

3. It is advisable to perform strength work with a training partner. Training partners are an invaluable help, not only with maintaining your motivation, but also with ensuring that you are adhering to strict form.

4. In each phase there is a recommended repetition range with a minimum and a maximum number. When starting the phase you should select a weight that allows you to perform the minimum number of repetitions and no more, no matter how hard you try. As you become stronger your repetitions will increase. Once you reach the maximum number of repetitions, increase the weight so that you can only perform the minimum number of repetitions. And so on.

5. When working with machines, ensure they are set up for your biomechanics. Most strength-training machines are fully adjustable. I know it can be time consuming to adjust the machines every time you use them, but it is a necessary evil when it comes to avoiding injury. Trying to fit into a machine that has been adjusted to suit someone else will place undesired forces on your joints, muscles and connective tissue and will result in an injury. Wherever possible, try to align your joints with the appropriate pivot on the machines.

6. Do not perform strength training on consecutive days; allow time for your muscles to recover and rebuild between workouts. If you are pushed for time, it is possible to perform strength workouts on two consecutive days, but only if you split your workouts into upper and lower body exercises. If you work your upper body one day, and then your lower body the next, no two body parts are stressed on both days.

7. Don't forget to breathe when you are exercising. Holding your breath whilst performing the exercises will only lead to dizziness. As a rule of thumb, breathe out on exertion and breathe in when relaxing. If this method does not suit you, just breathe normally as that is infinitely better for you than not breathing.

8. Youth category riders should only perform strength exercises using their body weight and should not perform weight training exercises.

9. Current research indicates that strength training causes muscles to shorten. In order to offset this potential problem, after your workout you should make sure that you perform the appropriate stretches for the muscles that you have been working.

STRENGTH TRAINING PROGRAMME

General Conditioning Phase

This is the first of your strength training phases and will last between 10 and 15 weeks. If you are new to weight lifting, or it has been some time since you last visited a gym, then it is wise to get some expert tuition for your first few visits to the weights room. Included here is a list of exercises that you should perform as part of this strength phase. If you are a veteran of the weights room and you already know your maximum strength for each of the exercises, the amount of weight that you will lift in this phase will be between 50 and 65 per cent of your maximum. You should perform between 15 and 20 repetitions of each exercise. If, however, you don't know your maximum strength in each exercise, I urge you not to try to find out. Lifting very heavy weights is an unnecessary injury risk; instead, you should use the first few visits to the gym to ascertain the correct weight so that you can perform the desired number of repetitions and no more. You should also use these first few workouts to concentrate on the correct lifting technique.

The strengthening exercises for this programme are designed in a circuit, with no body part worked on consecutive stations. This allows the fatigued muscles time to recover while the other muscles are working. You should perform one set on a particular exercise and then move straight on to the next exercise with little rest in between. It is designed like this in order to make efficient use of your time in the gym. It is not intended to give you any aerobic benefit. Your aerobic fitness level should easily be able to cope with the schedule without becoming unduly stressed.

You do not have to go to a specialist gym in order to strength train for mountain biking. It is possible to perform a wide range of strength exercises at home with the minimum of equipment. The basic equipment you need for an adequate home gym includes barbell, dumb-bells, bench, squat racks and chin-up bar. Even if you do train at a commercial gym, not all of the exercises, or the machines listed in this chapter, are going to be available to you. Where this is the case, replace the impractical exercises with similar ones that work the same muscles. There are many excellent books on the market, dedicated solely to weight training, that contain numerous strength exercises for you to choose from.

The Exercises
LEG EXTENSION

PURPOSE: This is an excellent exercise for isolating and developing the large muscle group on the front of the thigh (the quadriceps). This exercise also helps to prepare the quadriceps for the subsequent leg exercises.

PROCEDURE: Sit on the leg extension machine and place your feet under the padded rollers. Adjust the machine so that the axis of your knee is in line with the pivot on the machine.

Slowly extend your legs until they are straight, then pause momentarily in this position. You should be able to feel your quadriceps working.

Slowly lower the weight back to the starting position and repeat for the required number of repetitions.

EXERCISE TIPS: Keep your movements slow and deliberate.

Keep tension in your quadriceps throughout the entire range of the exercise by not putting the weight down. Initiate the upward phase of the movement before the cable goes slack. Do not allow the weights to bang together.

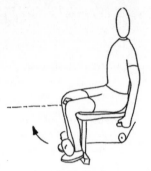

Leg extension

LEG CURL

PURPOSE: The exercise is the opposite of the one above. It strengthens and develops the large muscle group on the back of the thighs (the hamstrings) and when performed in conjunction with the leg extension it ensures proper muscle balance at the knee. This exercise also helps prepare the hamstrings for the subsequent leg exercises.

PROCEDURE: Lie face-down on the leg curl machine, and place your heels under the pads. Adjust your position so that the axis of your knee is in line with the pivot on the machine.

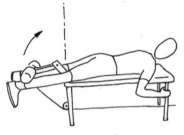

Leg curl

Slowly flex your legs and bring your heels as close to your buttocks as possible. Pause momentarily in this fully flexed position. You should be able to feel your hamstrings contracting.

Slowly lower the weight back to the starting position and repeat for the required number of repetitions.

EXERCISE TIPS: Move only at the knees. Do not select a weight that forces you to use your upper body and arch your back.

As with the leg extensions, keep tension in your muscles throughout the entire range of the exercise by not putting the weight down. Initiate the upward phase of the movement before the cable goes slack. Do not allow the weights to bang together.

LAT PULL-DOWNS

PURPOSE: Mountain biking requires a great deal of upper body strength. This exercise targets the large muscles on the upper back (the latissimus dorsi), the

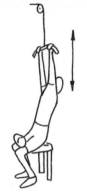

Lat pull-downs

rear of shoulders (the posterior deltoids) and the front of the upper arm (the biceps). It also helps improve your grip strength.

PROCEDURE: Take hold of the pull-down bar, with a slightly wider than shoulder-width overhand grip. Sit down on the machine and put your knees under the retainer pads.

Lean back slightly. Maintaining a slightly arched back, slowly and smoothly pull the bar down until it touches the top of your chest. Hold this position momentarily.

Slowly and smoothly return the bar to arm's length and feel the stretch in your muscles. Repeat for the desired number of repetitions.

EXERCISE TIPS: This exercise is most effective if you minimise any movement from the waist; the only body parts that should be moving are your arms.

For maximum effect, stretch the muscles at the top of every repetition.

SQUAT

PURPOSE: This is an ideal exercise for developing immense leg strength. It targets the muscles in the entire lower body, but it is the quadriceps that are affected the most.

Squat

PROCEDURE: Stand upright with your feet shoulder-width apart, a barbell resting across the back of your shoulders.

Keeping your head up and your back straight, slowly bend your knees until they are parallel to the floor.

Slowly push upwards, back to the starting position, and repeat for the required number of repetitions.

EXERCISE TIPS: Extra special care should be taken when performing squats due to the amount of strain placed on the vertebrae. Make sure you maintain a straight back at all times.

Throughout the exercise, make sure that your knees stay over, and in line with, your feet at all times.

Do not allow your knees to splay outwards, or let them go below 90°.

It is a good idea to perform this exercise in front of a full-length mirror so that you can keep an eye on your technique at all times.

This exercise can be made more comfortable if you place a low block of wood under your heels.

SEATED ROWS

PURPOSE: This is another great exercise for targeting the large muscles of the upper back (the latissimus dorsi). It also develops the rear of the shoulders (the posterior deltoids) and the front of the upper arm (biceps) and it also helps improve your grip strength.

PROCEDURE: Sit down on the seated row machine. Place your feet on the foot plates, and have a slight bend in your knees.

Seated rows

Take hold of the handle and slowly pull it towards your abdominals. At the same time arch your back. Throughout the exercise, do not lean too far forwards or backwards.

Slowly return to the starting position, lowering the weight until you feel a stretch in your latissimus muscles. Repeat for the required number of repetitions.

EXERCISE TIPS: You can make this exercise more mountain bike specific by using a grip width which is similar to that on your mountain bike.

With some machines it is possible to change the type of bar that you can use. If this is the case at your gym, alternate with a bar that allows a vertical grip similar to that of pulling back on bar ends.

LEG PRESS

PURPOSE: This exercise develops the same muscles as the squat, but because of its range of motion, the action is similar to pushing down on a pedal.

PROCEDURE: Sit in the leg press machine, and place your feet shoulder-width apart on the foot plate.

Remove the safety bars, bend your knees and slowly lower the weight.

When your knees are bent at right angles, slowly press the weight back to the starting position. Repeat for the required number of repetitions.

EXERCISE TIPS: Keep the tension in your legs throughout the full range of movement by not locking your knees out.

Leg press

Vary your foot position in each workout.

Shoulder-width apart develops all-round leg strength. A closer foot position targets the outer thigh, while a slightly wider foot position develops the inner thigh.

BENCH PRESS

PURPOSE: The bench press develops the large muscles on the chest (pectoral muscles), the muscles on the front of the shoulders (the anterior deltoids) and the back of the upper arm (the triceps).

Bench press

PROCEDURE: Lie face up on a bench that is equipped with racks. Take hold of the barbell a little wider than shoulder-width apart. Press the barbell off the rack.

Slowly lower the weight until it touches your lower pectoral muscles. Ensure that throughout the execution of this exercise your elbows are pointing outwards.

Slowly press the weight back to the starting position. Repeat for the required number of repetitions.

EXERCISE TIPS: Keep your elbows out to the sides throughout the movement and keep your wrists directly above your elbows.

Do not arch your back.

Do not bounce the weight on your chest in order to get extra momentum.

CALF RAISE

PURPOSE: This exercise isolates the calf muscles (gastrocnemius) and is an excellent way to develop their dynamic strength.

PROCEDURE: Stand on your toes on the blocks of the calf raise machine. Place your shoulders under the pads.

Keeping your back straight, and your knees slightly bent, slowly raise up onto the balls of your feet. Hold this position momentarily and feel the contraction in your calves.

Slowly lower your heels as far as possible and hold this position momentarily. You should feel a stretching sensation within the calves.

Slowly press the weight back to the starting position and repeat for the required number of repetitions.

Calf raise

EXERCISE TIPS: Only use your calf muscles to lift the weight. Do not use body movements to help generate momentum.

Ensure that your range of motion is from full stretch at the bottom to fully contracted at the top.

Keep your back straight and your knees slightly bent.

SIDE LATERALS

PURPOSE: This exercise develops the middle of the shoulder muscles (medial deltoids), and contributes greatly to your upper body strength.

PROCEDURE: Stand upright with your arms down at your sides, and a dumb-bell in each hand.

With a slight bend in your elbows, slowly raise your arms out to your sides in a big arc. Lift the weights to a point slightly higher than your shoulders.

Slowly lower the weights to the starting position and repeat for the required number of repetitions.

EXERCISE TIP: Ensure that you are lifting the dumb-bells straight out to the sides and not too far forwards or backwards.

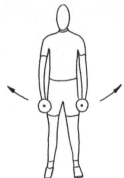

Side laterals

BICEPS CURL

PURPOSE: The biceps curl works the muscle on the front of your upper arm (the biceps) and helps develop your grip strength.

PROCEDURE: Stand upright with your feet about shoulder-width apart. Take hold of a barbell with an underhand grip. Your grip should also be shoulder-width apart and the barbell should be touching the tops of your thighs.

Without moving your upper arm, slowly curl the weight upwards in an arc. Ensure that your wrists remain fixed throughout the exercise.

Pause momentarily at the top and feel the contraction in your biceps muscles.

Biceps curl

Slowly lower to the starting position and repeat for the required number of repetitions.

EXERCISE TIP: This is an easy exercise in which to cheat the weight up. Ensure that you have strict form and that you are not giving the barbell any momentum by moving your upper body.

TRICEPS EXTENSION

PURPOSE: This exercise is the opposite of the previous one. The triceps extension develops the muscles on the back of your upper arm (the triceps). Your triceps muscles are

Triceps extension

worked a lot during technical descents when your arms are used to absorb the impact of the trail.

PROCEDURE: Stand in front of a triceps extension machine. Take hold of the bar with a shoulder width grip and with both elbows flexed.

Keeping your upper arm parallel to your body, slowly extend your arms down towards the floor.

Pause momentarily in the fully extended position and feel the contraction in your triceps muscles.

Slowly return to the start and repeat for the required number of repetitions.

EXERCISE TIPS: Only allow your elbow to bend to 90°.

To isolate the triceps muscles, keep your elbows tucked in to your sides.

SIT-UPS

PURPOSE: Sit-ups develop your stomach muscles (abdominals). As we have seen, mountain biking does not work the abdominals much and as a result they are

Sit-ups

comparatively weak. This exercise brings these muscles up to par and helps improve posture.

PROCEDURE: Lie face-up on a comfortable mat. Bend your knees and place your feet flat on the floor. Place your hands on the back of your head.

Slowly curl your torso up to meet your knees.

Pause momentarily in the contracted position, and slowly return to the start.

Repeat for the required number of repetitions.

EXERCISE TIPS: Keep this exercise ultra slow and focus on your abdominals throughout the whole exercise.

Keep your lower back on the floor at all times.

SIDE BENDS

PURPOSE: Side bends work the sides of your torso (the oblique muscles). They are important muscles involved in manoeuvring the bike and maintaining correct riding posture.

PROCEDURE: Stand upright with your feet shoulder-width apart. Hold a dumb-bell in your right hand and place your left hand on the back of your head.

Slowly bend over to your right side and feel the stretch.

Return to the start position. After the desired number of repetitions, repeat with the other side.

EXERCISE TIPS: Throughout the exercise, make sure that you bend to the side only and not too far forwards or backwards.

This exercise can be made more intense by holding a weight in your free hand.

Side bends

Power and Strength Phase

Following the conditioning phase, you should make your transition to the power and strength stage. This should coincide with your preparation phases P1 and P2 (see chapter eight) and should last up to 15 weeks. In this phase there is an increase in the number of sets (3 to 5), an increase in weight and a subsequent reduction in the number of repetitions (12 to 8).

It is important to note that during this phase the intensity of the exercise is high and as such there is increased stress on the muscles, tendons, ligaments and joints. Great care must be taken whilst you are performing these exercises as an injury now, so close to the race season, could drastically effect your peak performance. If you feel any discomfort whatsoever, back off and reduce the weight and sets and increase the repetitions. Always employ caution.

You should perform the same circuits as in the conditioning phase with the corresponding changes in exercise intensity and duration. This is a long phase and the exercises can quickly feel repetitive and uninteresting. To prevent yourself from becoming stale and unmotivated vary your training. You can spice up your strength training programme in many ways. The most popular methods include:

1. Alternate your workouts with barbell and dumb-bell exercises;
2. Workout with a training partner;
3. Occasionally visit a new gym;
4. Swap the exercises round;
5. Introduce new exercises to the programme.

Muscular Endurance

For the final three or four weeks of your P2 phase (see chapter eight) it is time to work on muscular endurance. You should follow this programme up to the beginning of your competition or peak phase. The sets during this phase will be reduced back to two and there will be an increase in repetitions (20 to 25) with an accompanying reduction in weight. In order to maximise the endurance of the muscles, rest periods between sets will be reduced to a minimum (30 seconds). Because of the extended duration of the sets and the close proximity of the racing season, the total number of exercises will be reduced. Choose your favourite exercise for each body part and incorporate them into a workout.

During the peak phase there will be a great demand placed upon your body as a result of the racing schedule. The key to success and longevity during this phase is maintenance. A tough strength training regime during this phase could easily facilitate the onset of over-reaching and eventually over-training – which may eventually bring about the downfall of your racing season.

During the race season you should use the muscular endurance programme, but you must always exercise common sense with your strength training during this period. If you have a schedule where there are a lot of race dates in close proximity, back off on your strength training and focus upon recovering fully between each race. If your race calendar depicts that one month there are very few races then it would be prudent to include some strength-maintenance training into your programme.

ALTERNATIVE STRENGTH TRAINING METHODS

For one reason or another, you may not be able to get to a gym to do your strength training. This may be because you are pushed for time, stuck at work, travelling, or on holiday. However, this does not mean that you have to cancel your workout, because it is possible to perform an effective strength workout with little or no equipment.

There is a handy strength training device on the market which I advise every mountain biker to have. It is manufactured by Reebok and is basically a length of rubber cord with a handle at either end. This simple gadget allows you to perform numerous upper and lower body exercises, and when it is combined with supplementary bodyweight exercises such as sit-ups, press-ups, lunges and squats, you can get an effective strength workout done.

Strength Circuit

If you are a youth rider and are avoiding training with weights, or if you just fancy a change from your usual programme, you may wish to perform some circuit training. The following circuit can be performed with no equipment.

PRESS-UPS

PURPOSE: This exercise is a body weight version of the bench press. It develops the large muscles on the front of the chest (the pectorals), the muscles on the front of the shoulders (the anterior deltoids) and the back of the upper arm (the triceps).

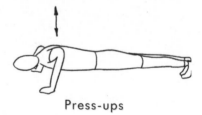

Press-ups

PROCEDURE: Lie face down on the floor. Your hands should be next to your shoulders with your palms flat on the floor. Your back should be straight and your feet should be shoulder-width apart.

Keeping a straight back, push yourself upwards until your arms are almost straight.

Slowly lower yourself until the tip of your nose touches the floor, then repeat the procedure.

EXERCISE TIP: Vary your hand position to target different areas. A wide hand-span works the pectoral muscles, whereas a close hand-span works the triceps.

CALF RAISES

PURPOSE: This exercise isolates the calf muscles (gastrocnemius) and is an excellent way to develop their dynamic strength.

PROCEDURE: Stand on your left leg and bend your right leg. You will need to hold onto an immovable object for support.

Now raise up onto the ball of your left leg and feel the contraction in your left calf muscle.

Slowly lower yourself back down and repeat the procedure.

EXERCISE TIP: Remember to do the same number of repetitions for the right leg.

Calf raises

BODYWEIGHT SQUATS

PURPOSE: This is an ideal exercise for developing all-round leg strength. It targets the muscles in the entire lower body, but it is the quadriceps that are affected the most.

PROCEDURE: Stand upright with your feet shoulder-width apart.

Keeping your head up and your back straight, slowly bend your knees until they are parallel to the floor.

Slowly push upwards, back to the starting position, and repeat the procedure.

EXERCISE TIPS: Make sure that your knees stay over, and in line with, your feet at all times.

Do not allow your knees to splay outwards.

This exercise can be made more comfortable if you place a low block of wood under your heels.

Bodyweight squats

SIT-UPS

PURPOSE: Sit-ups develop your stomach muscles (abdominals). As we have seen, mountain biking does not work the abdominals much and as a result they are comparatively weak. This exercise brings these muscles up to par and helps improve posture.

PROCEDURE: Lie face-up on a comfortable mat. Bend your knees and place your feet flat on the floor. Place your hands on the back of your head.

Sit-ups

Slowly curl your torso up to meet your knees. Aim to keep your lower back on the floor at all times.

Pause momentarily in the contracted position and slowly return to the start.

Repeat for the required number of repetitions.

EXERCISE TIPS: Keep this exercise ultra slow and focus on your abdominals throughout the whole exercise.

Keep your lower back on the floor at all times.

LOWER BACK RAISES

PURPOSE: The lower back muscles are crucial in mountain biking in order to maintain correct riding posture.

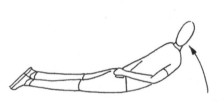

PROCEDURE: Lie face-down on a mat. Place your hands (palms up) on your lower back.

Keeping your hips and legs on the floor, raise your torso as high off the mat as possible.

Slowly return to the start position and repeat the procedure.

Lower back raises

EXERCISE TIPS: Don't strain your neck in the upward phase. Look straight ahead. Hold the contracted position before lowering.

As you become stronger, shift your bodyweight forwards by placing your fingers on your temples.

TRICEPS DIPS

PURPOSE: Triceps dips develop the muscles on the back of your upper arm (the triceps). Your triceps muscles are worked a lot during technical descents when your arms are used to absorb the impact of the trail.

PROCEDURE: Sit down with your back to a bench. Place your palms on the bench, shoulder-width apart and fingers facing forward.

Slowly press your body up and feel the contraction in the triceps.

Slowly lower yourself and repeat the procedure.

Triceps dips

EXERCISE TIPS: This exercise can be made easier by bending your knees.

To maintain tension in the triceps, do not lock out your elbows at the top of the movement.

SIMULATED CHIN-UPS

PURPOSE: This exercise helps develop the large muscles on the upper back (the latissimus dorsi and the rhomboid muscles).

PROCEDURE: Lie face-down on a mat with your arm out to your sides.

Bend your elbows 90°. Raise your arms off the mat and squeeze your shoulder blades together.

Continuously simulate a chin-up movement with your arms.

EXERCISE TIPS: Perform the movements slowly and purposefully.

Simulated chin-ups

Keep the shoulder blade retracted throughout the movement.

You should perform each exercise for one minute and then move immediately on to the next exercise. Once you have completed all the exercises, rest for two minutes then repeat the circuit two more times.

7. FURTHER TRAINING METHODS

HEART-RATE TRAINING ZONES

Just as a machine is composed of smaller, individual working parts, a properly designed mountain bike fitness programme consists of many separate training workouts. Each one of these specific workouts targets a specific area of your fitness and has a crucial, synergistic role in the overall development of your mountain bike fitness.

To ensure that you reach the required intensity to evoke the desired training response, the workout protocols listed in this chapter are accompanied by heart-rate (HR) targets. These targets are individual and are based upon your heart-rate reserve (HRR). In order to calculate your HRR use the following equation:

$$HRR = \text{Heart Rate (max)} - \text{Heart Rate (rest)}$$

This value is then used to calculate your HR target.

$$HR \text{ (target)} = HR \text{ (rest)} + \% \text{ intensity x } HRR$$

Table 6: Heart-rate Training Zones

% INTENSITY	TYPE OF TRAINING
90+ =	Maximal Training Intensity (MaxTI)
85–90 =	Anaerobic Training Intensity (AnTI)
80–85 =	Aerobic Power (AP)
70–80 =	Steady State Training Intensity (SSTI)
60–70 =	Aerobic Training Intensity (AeTI)
<60 =	Moderate Training Intensity (ModTI)

ANAEROBIC THRESHOLD TRAINING

The area of training that will have the single most profound effect on your mountain bike performance is anaerobic threshold training. But, before we go any further, it is important to have an overview of the different systems that are employed in order to produce the energy that is required for mountain biking. Our energy originally comes from the food that we eat. This nutrient energy is converted, either *aerobically* (with oxygen) or *anaerobically* (without oxygen) into useable energy via our energy systems (see chapter one).

As the intensity of exercise increases and the demand for energy rises, there is a point where the predominant energy system swaps over from the aerobic energy system to the anaerobic energy system, and as a result lactic acid accumulates. The point where this exchange occurs is inter-specific. It is different from rider to rider, but for trained athletes it is typically in the region of 85 to 95 per cent of their maximum heart rate. However, an estimate or prediction falls short of the mark for the serious mountain biker because an error either way can mean the facilitation of fatigue or the failure to attain optimum performance.

Lactic acid is the by-product of anaerobic exercise, but in the presence of oxygen it is metabolised further to yield more energy. As such it is strictly speaking not a waste product. The problem occurs when the oxygen supply fails to meet the demand for energy. As a result, lactic acid production outstrips its rate of metabolism and it begins to accumulate. This is accompanied by a burning sensation in the muscles which is typically associated with performing hard work such as sprints or climbs.

Because the information you require is 'under your skin', the majority of anaerobic threshold tests are invasive. An anaerobic threshold test performed at a sports medicine laboratory involves numerous blood samples to be taken during incremental exercise, which are subsequently analysed for blood lactate concentrations.

Due to the invasive nature, and the equipment required for a laboratory test, it is little wonder that they are expensive and inconvenient. Fortunately there is an alternative method which only requires a resistance trainer and a heart-rate monitor – both of which are prerequisites of the serious mountain bikers' training tool kit.

To meet the demands of increased physical activity, the heart beats more frequently and increases the supply of blood to the working muscles. This vital blood supply transports fuel and oxygen to the working muscles and relieves them of the detrimental toxic by-products. If you graph your heart rate and exercise intensity, it becomes apparent that there is a positive linear relationship between the two. This correlation continues up to a point, then the heart rate levels off despite increases in exercise intensity. This relationship forms the basis of the anaerobic threshold test and can easily be used to determine your anaerobic threshold. The test is advantageous in that it does not require blood samples: it can be performed with minimal equipment and is therefore inexpensive and more convenient than a laboratory test.

Test for Determining Anaerobic Threshold

PURPOSE: The purpose of this test is to ascertain your anaerobic threshold and your corresponding heart rate. This heart-rate information is important because you can use it to determine whether or not you are producing lactic acid at a rate that outstrips your ability to remove it. If you go above your anaerobic threshold you will accumulate lactic acid, which will eventually be detrimental to your mountain bike performance. If you stray too far below it, you won't be accumulating lactic acid, but neither will you be putting in a good performance time. Ideally you should strike a balance between the two.

PROTOCOL: The protocol for the anaerobic threshold test is straightforward and easy to administer. Following a warm-up (see chapter four), commence the test with a starting resistance in the region of 150 watts. There is no exact starting resistance, as this depends on your individual fitness. What might be 'easy' for one rider might fatigue another. If in doubt, err on the side of caution and select a resistance that is too easy. This is preferred over a difficult starting resistance, as the latter will reduce the number of data points. Every minute, increase the resistance, by 10 watts and make a note of the resistance and your heart rate each minute. It is important to maintain a steady cadence throughout the test. You may select your own preferred pedal frequency, but you must maintain this for the duration of the test.

TESTING TIPS: This is a very demanding test, so make sure that you are fully prepared for it both mentally and physically.

Ask someone to assist you with the test and record all of the data. In the interests of safety, it is good practice to have someone at hand especially when you are performing such an intense test.

The next step is to plot the data (intensity against heart rate), either manually or automatically via a heart-rate monitor that is compatible with a personal computer. Connect the points with a straight line, or get your software package to do so, and examine the graph for the point of deflection. Make a note of the corresponding heart rate and power output.

Alternatively you can work with speed instead of power. The protocol of the test remains the same, except that you increase the speed by 1.5 kmh (approximately 1 mph) every minute until exhaustion.

Diagram 5: Anaerobic Threshold Test Performed on a Cycle Ergometer

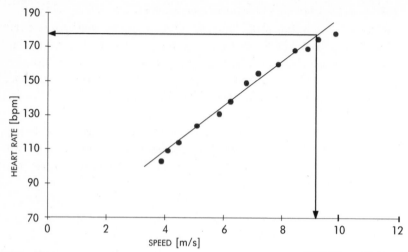

In the above example the rider's heart rate follows a linear pattern as the speed is increased. This relationship continues until a speed of 9 m/s is reached and then, when further increases in speed are performed, the heart rate deflects. For this particular rider the anaerobic threshold is about 177 beats per minute (bpm). In real terms this means that if he exercises at an intensity that raises his heart rate above 177, he will be producing lactic acid which may result in fatigue. If, however, the rider reduces his heart rate significantly below 177 bpm, he will not be exercising at his optimum. The key is to race as close to your anaerobic threshold as possible, rarely going above it for prolonged periods of time.

The effects of training your anaerobic threshold concern these two values. The training effect will increase your heart rate at anaerobic threshold, but only to a certain point, and then it will level out. However, with continued training at anaerobic threshold, you will notice an increased power output at your anaerobic threshold heart rate. In mountain biking terms this means that you will be able to ride at a faster pace before lactic acid accumulates.

Training above your anaerobic threshold requires intense work at high percentages of your maximum heart rate and involves short repeated bouts of intense training punctuated by recovery periods. This type of training is affectionately known as interval training. Before I elaborate on the training protocols for enhancing your anaerobic threshold, I cannot overstate the importance of ensuring that you warm-up and recover thoroughly – more so because of the high intensity and stress that this type of training places on your body.

Time Trial Anaerobic Threshold Test

PURPOSE: The purpose of this test is to ascertain your anaerobic threshold heart rate. It requires very little equipment and is relatively accurate.

PROCEDURE: This test is nothing more than recording your average heart rate during a time trial (10 miles produces an accurate result). By definition, a time trial involves covering a set distance in the quickest possible time. For the test it is important that you maintain a constant speed for the entire time trial. Your average heart rate for the time trial will be within a few beats of your anaerobic threshold.

TESTING TIP: Perform this test as part of a workout and not during a race. The race results will typically give a higher than normal anaerobic threshold as you will no doubt tolerate the accumulating lactic acid more because of the race atmosphere and the flowing adrenaline.

Anaerobic Threshold Workouts (ATW)

The anaerobic threshold workouts are designed to increase your heart rate at anaerobic threshold. When performed correctly they will also increase your power output for a set anaerobic threshold heart rate.

ATW1

PURPOSE: The purpose of ATW1 is to overload your energy systems by working above your anaerobic threshold for extended periods of time.

PROCEDURE: ATW1 is in essence the purest form of anaerobic threshold training. It involves working at a zone that is a few beats above your anaerobic threshold for at least 5 minutes. Build up intensity gradually until you reach the heart rate that is slightly above your anaerobic threshold and maintain it for at least 5 minutes.

WORKOUT TIP: When performing this test it is helpful to have a heart-rate monitor with a training zone facility. Set your alarm to go off when you go above your anaerobic threshold and then try to keep going for 5 minutes.

ATW2

PURPOSE: The purpose of ATW2 is similar to that of the previous workout, except that the workout is more race specific.

PROCEDURE: ATW2 involves simulating a race with your riding partners. You should ride intensely, but ensure that you do not go above your threshold heart rate by more than 5 beats per minute. It is okay to drop a few beats below – in fact you will probably need to – but by the end of the session you should have spent a cumulative 30 to 40 minutes at your anaerobic threshold.

WORKOUT TIP: It can often be difficult to keep track of the intensity at which you are working. There is a distinct advantage having a heart-rate monitor with a memory recall facility, so that you can analyse your training afterwards and make any necessary adjustments for future workouts.

Anaerobic Threshold and VO_2 Max

We first touched on the relationship between anaerobic threshold and VO_2 max in chapter one. As you will remember, VO_2 max is the maximum volume of oxygen that an athlete can absorb and use, and it is often used to assess his fitness. It is argued that anaerobic threshold is a better predictor of athletic performance. This is because the onset of blood lactate accumulation (OBLA) begins at higher levels of oxygen consumption for trained riders than it does for untrained ones. Moreover, as a result of training, you can increase your anaerobic threshold without a commensurate increase in your VO_2 max. Therefore, in this scenario, if you were to measure your fitness in terms of VO_2 max, your test results would indicate that you have not improved, when in reality you have done.

Diagram 6: The Relationship between Anaerobic Threshold and VO_2 Max

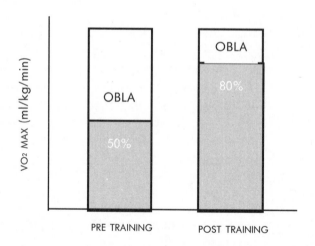

The above graph illustrates the dynamics between VO_2 max and anaerobic threshold for a hypothetical rider. In this situation there is no difference in VO_2 max following training, yet there is a significant increase at the point of OBLA. Therefore anaerobic threshold is a more sensitive measure of the rider's performance.

INTERVAL TRAINING

Interval training is the term given to the mode of exercise which involves performing a series of intense exercise bouts that are punctuated with less concentrated sections, or relief periods. Done correctly, interval training will allow you to perform a greater volume of intense work per training session than if you were to train continually at a similar intensity with no recovery.

Diagram 7: Heart Rate Response to Interval Training

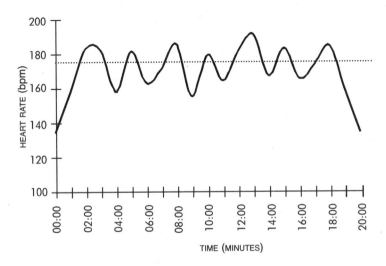

TIME (MINUTES)

Diagram 7 shows a hypothetical interval-training heart-rate response for a mountain biker whose anaerobic threshold is 175 bpm (the anaerobic threshold is represented by the dotted line). In the above example, the cumulative time spent above 175 bpm is greater than that if the rider had ridden intensely from the outset without any rest periods.

In addition, interval training is an excellent tool for increasing speed. Not just riding speed, but also limb speed. In mountain biking, leg speed is closely associated with cadence and pedalling efficiency. Interval training can effectively be used to improve your ability to increase your cadence suddenly, which in turn will greatly improve your ability to accelerate. When your intervals are of short duration, say 30 seconds, there is very little time to move up through the gears; and even if you did have the time, big gears would be cumbersome and would hinder your ability to accelerate. It is therefore an advantage to be able to increase your cadence suddenly and accelerate rapidly in a relatively low gear.

With careful manipulation of the exercise intensity, duration and the relief periods, you can tailor the workout to meet your demands. Intense, short-duration work periods with relatively long relief sections will enhance your explosive speed and your cadence and also develop your phosphocreatine energy system. If you reduce the intensity of the work periods and increase their duration, you will be improving your ability to tolerate hard exercise for prolonged periods of time.

The Workouts
ACCELERATION SPRINTS

PURPOSE: Having the ability to perform acceleration sprints is a very useful resource in your mountain biking repertoire. Acceleration sprints involve increasing your speed from a rolling start, to a moderate fast pace, to a fast pace, all the way up to maximal effort. Acceleration sprints are often required at the end of a race when there is a dash to the line. Here the ability to maintain (and increase) pace over a period of time is of paramount importance if you are to notch up a better finishing position. Quite often during a race you may need to call on acceleration sprints in order to outmanoeuvre a competitor and reach a certain point of the course first. An example of this is beating your opponents to an area of single track where it is then difficult for them to overtake.

PROCEDURE: For this workout you will need a long, flat, off-road section on which to train. You will need to have a 150-metre stretch of ground with plenty of run-off. Approach the 'start' at a relatively easy pace. As you pass the start, change up a few gears and work at a moderately hard pace for 50 metres. Then change up again and ride at a fast pace for the next 50 metres. As you enter the final 50-metre stretch, sprint maximally to the 'finish'. Cycle back to the start at a very easy pace and recover until your heart rate drops to Aerobic Training Intensity (AeTI).

Diagram 8: Acceleration Sprints

START	MODERATE	HARD →	MAXIMUM	FINISH
	→		→	

WORKOUT TIPS: Before you start, have visual markers to indicate the transition period. Lamp-posts or trees are ideal for this.

When training for acceleration, it is important that you do not think of it in terms of 50-metre 'blocks'. Instead, you should visualise yourself as building up momentum smoothly over a distance until eventually you are working maximally.

In order to allow for progressive overload you can: increase the number of sets (one complete acceleration sprint is one set – perform no more than 10 per workout); increase the distance of each phase; or decrease the rest interval between sets.

HOLLOW SPRINTS

PURPOSE: Hollow sprints train your body to use less effort while sprinting; they teach your body to work in 'economy' mode. This technique can be useful when cycling fast in a bunch of riders.

PROCEDURE: From a rolling start, sprint maximally out of your saddle for 50 metres, then for the next 50 metres sit back in the saddle and maintain your pace and momentum whilst consciously trying to use less energy. Then, for the final 50 metres sprint maximally out of the saddle again. Cycle back to the start at a very easy pace and recover until your heart rate drops to AeTI.

WORKOUT TIPS: Before you start, have visual markers to indicate the transition period. Lamp-posts or trees are ideal for this.

During the middle 50 metres concentrate on pedal technique and relax those muscles not involved in sprinting.

A good technique is to think 'jelly jaw'. If you concentrate on relaxing your jaw muscles, many of the other muscles not involved with sprinting will relax. It is a technique used by world-class 100-metre sprinters and if it works for them, it should work for you.

SPRINT INTERVALS

PURPOSE: Sprint intervals are an excellent way of increasing your tolerance to the build-up of blood lactate that is associated with hard, fast riding. This type of sprinting may be necessary in a race scenario when you are trying to lose a competitor. When two riders are locked in battle like this, it is the one with superior lactate tolerance who is usually the victor.

PROCEDURE: Because this is a high-intensity workout you should warm up thoroughly for about 30 minutes in advance. When you are ready, ride for 2 minutes at Maximum Training Intensity (MaxTI), immediately followed by 2 minutes at AeTI. Recover by riding easy for 15 minutes, then repeat the whole procedure two more times (with a 15-minute cool-down between each set).

WORKOUT TIPS: This is a tough workout, both mentally and physically. Before attempting it you need to be in a fully recovered state and be raring to go.

The workout can be made more interesting by introducing some competition. Have a rider of similar ability train with you. Ride in single file with your training partner about 10 metres behind you. As soon as your partner sees you make your move and initiate the sprint, he has to try to catch up and overtake you within two minutes. Your job, of course, is to out-sprint your partner. For the next sprint, change roles.

DECREASING INTERVALS

PURPOSE: Decreasing intervals train your body to perform a number of repeated maximal sprints with minimum amount of recovery time. In a racing scenario it is a distinct advantage to be able to sprint just as well towards the end of the race as you could at the beginning.

PROCEDURE: Again, this is a high-intensity workout, so you should warm up thoroughly for about 30 minutes beforehand. When you feel ready, sprint as hard as you can for one minute. If you are performing the sprint correctly, you should not be able to maintain the speed for any longer than 60 seconds. Recover and ride easy until your heart rate drops to AeTI. Once this heart rate is achieved, immediately sprint as hard as you can for 50 seconds. Recover once again until your heart rate drops to AeTI and then sprint for 40 seconds, recover . . . and so on until your final sprint is for 10 seconds.

WORKOUT TIP: This is a tough workout, both mentally and physically. Before attempting it you need to be in a fully recovered state and be raring to go.

Because of the rigid timing structure, this exercise lends itself to being performed on a resistance trainer with an assistant to monitor your time.

CLIMBING INTERVALS

PURPOSE: For obvious reasons this workout is really only pertinent to the cross-country mountain biker. During the course of a cross-country race, riders are required to ride hard up short duration hills many times. This is physically demanding and your competitors will cut you no slack. If you can climb well then you will have a distinct advantage over your cohorts. After all, there must be some substance to the old cross-country adage that 'many a race is won on the climbs'. The climbing intervals workout described below is a great way to improve your ability to repeatedly ride hard up tough climbs.

PROCEDURE: Following a thorough warm-up of at least 30 minutes' duration, climb as hard as possible up a hill (no more than 3 km). Don't slow down as you approach the top; instead, try to ride even faster the further you go. Once you reach the top, turn around and ride back down and recover. Keep turning the cranks on the descent in order to keep the blood flowing to your legs. If you haven't recovered by the time you get to the bottom (your heart rate should be near AeTI) do a few loops at the foot of the climb if necessary. Repeat the procedure as many times as you can (no more than 10). As you become increasingly fatigued, you don't have to climb the same height on each repetition. Ride three quarters of the way up, then halfway and so on.

WORKOUT TIPS: Use different climbing techniques, for instance in the saddle and out of the saddle.

Try to go faster, the higher up the hill you get.

Vary your procedure. For instance, on some occasions you may start sprinting in a low gear with a high cadence, and then halfway up the climb, change up (yes up) a gear and then up once more near the top. It's easy to stick with someone on a climb if you are in a low gear: when they struggle and change down, you change up, pull away change up again and power through and over the top of the climb – don't slow down like everyone else.

FARTLEK TRAINING

Fartlek training is a gift to anyone following a long-term training programme as it can often inject a breath of fresh air in an otherwise monotonous regime. Fartlek is a Swedish term which means 'speed play' and was popularised by Swedish Olympic coach Gosta Holmer as an effective training protocol. Fartlek training borrows heavily from the interval style of training, but offers more flexibility and freedom due to the absence of a rigid framework. In other words, the session is informal yet still initiates a training response.

Because of the lack of structure, this form of training is ideally suited to off-road riding. In contrast to interval training, fartlek training is not tied to a structure of pre-determined work and relief periods. Instead the intensity is depicted by the terrain and by you. You ride hard when you are faced with something that requires you to ride hard, like a tough climb or a stretch of fast single-track. And you ride easy when the terrain dictates, for instance when there is a technical section that needs to be ridden slowly, or there is a gentle sweeping downhill.

This form of training allows for the typical long-weekend ride to be slotted into your training plan. Throughout the course of a long mountain bike ride, your heart rate will fluctuate widely. It is highly unlikely that this heart-rate trace will fit into a rigid interval schedule. Fortunately, the concept behind fartlek training acknowledges that there are significant fitness benefits to be had from a random mix of intensities that don't happen to fit into a rigid framework.

This particular form of training is of great benefit to the mountain biker, as it allows for an additional degree of specificity. It can sometimes be difficult to perform precise interval training off-road due to the undulating terrain. You may find with intervals that the time-scale requires you to sprint, but the terrain is a downhill; or that you should be resting but you are on a steep climb. Fartlek training allows you to perform your intervals off-road. You may decide to work hard on the climbs and recover on the downhill, or sprint along sections of single track and coast on the fire roads, or sprint from one tree to the next, then recover and repeat. Throughout the entire workout you should vary the intensity and pace based on how you feel, what the terrain is like, and what you want to accomplish. The permutations are limitless.

However, some caution must be exercised and you shouldn't get too carried away with fartlek training. Unless you know the terrain well, it is easy to work too hard. If you have a scheduled recovery ride with a ceiling-limit heart rate (a heart-rate limit that you cannot go above), it is wise to avoid fartlek training altogether. For instance, you might encounter a prolonged hill which would elevate your heart rate above your threshold, rendering the workout at best useless and at worst detrimental to your performance. The price to pay for the unpredictability of fartlek exercise is that it is often difficult to monitor your training. Ideally you should have a programmable heart-rate monitor so that you can analyse the time spent at various intensity levels afterwards.

It is best to use this form of training towards the end of your foundation phase and during your peak preparation phase, because it is an ideal way to introduce intense intervals into your programme. It's also a good way of putting them into practice off-road. That said, you can perform fartlek training at any time especially if you feel that you are getting into a training rut and want to add a bit of flavour to your workouts.

The Workout

PURPOSE: This workout adds an element of fun to your training. It develops several of your fitness components at once and enhances all of your energy systems.

PROCEDURE: Start off riding easy for 10 minutes (easy intensity). This phase can be part of your warm-up.

For the next 30 minutes, ride up every hill you encounter at an even pace (medium intensity). Try to stay in your middle ring.

After each hill, ride slowly and try to bring your heart rate down to AeTI (easy intensity) for two minutes. This may mean that you have to ride very slowly or even do a track-stand if the terrain won't allow for easy riding.

Ride at an even pace and look out for some natural markers (e.g. trees) that are 50 to 60 metres apart. Then perform six sprint repeats (difficult intensity) with one minute of recovery in between.

Following the sprints, ride easy and try to bring your heart rate down to AeTI (easy intensity) for two minutes. This may mean that you have to do a track-stand if the terrain won't allow for easy riding.

Ride the terrain at race pace for the next 10 minutes (moderate/difficult intensity)

Finish off riding easy for 10 minutes (easy intensity). This phase can be part of your cool-down.

WORKOUT TIPS: You can devise you own workout beforehand or make it up as you go along.

Make sure to include all of the intensities: easy, medium and difficult.

AEROBIC ENDURANCE

For the mountain biker, aerobic endurance is chiefly concerned with being able to maintain a riding pace that is predominantly aerobic. This has two main benefits. Firstly, it trains the aerobic energy system to use fats as its preferred fuel, thereby conserving valuable carbohydrates. Secondly, by the very nature of aerobic metabolism, lactic acid is not produced.

The Workout
PURPOSE: The maximum amount of energy per unit time that you are able to produce aerobically is known as your aerobic power. To a large extent this value is dependent upon your cardio-respiratory and aerobic energy systems. Both of these components can be enhanced as a result of correct aerobic training.

PROCEDURE: In order for aerobic training to be effective, you must exercise within your aerobic training zone. Your aerobic training zone lies within your aerobic and anaerobic thresholds. Your aerobic threshold is the minimum workload that will initiate a training effect – below this there will be no observable adaptations. The ceiling limit is your anaerobic threshold, above which you will predominantly be using your anaerobic energy system and producing lactic acid as a by-product.

WORKOUT TIPS: To calculate the corresponding heart rate use the chart in chapter nine.

The minimum duration of the workout should be one hour. The maximum time spent in this zone is dependent on your fitness and mountain bike discipline. It is not uncommon for ultra-distance riders to train for up to eight hours in this zone.

Aerobic System Test
PURPOSE: You should use this test to ascertain your aerobic power and then use it to monitor the progress of your aerobic system.

PROCEDURE: For this test you will need to use a resistance trainer in a gym, or better still you can set your bike up on an indoor trainer. You should prime your cardio-respiratory system by warming up thoroughly before you commence the test. Then ride for 5 miles at a steady target heart rate which is below your anaerobic threshold. Record the time that it took to complete the distance.

TESTING TIPS: To maintain accuracy, it is important that you stay within a couple of beats of your target heart rate.

You should use the test throughout your training programme to assess your aerobic status. The fitter you are, the quicker your time will be for the given heart rate.

PLYOMETRIC TRAINING

Plyometric exercise is a relative newcomer to the world of physical fitness training. It is a form of training that targets and enhances the fitness components that produce instantaneous power, or sudden bursts of energy – traits that are repeatedly required in competitive mountain biking. Leg power is needed for quick sprints, jumps and quick manoeuvres. As such it is important that all mountain bikers incorporate plyometric training into their training schedules in order to achieve complete development. However, plyometric training is especially pertinent to downhill mountain bikers and dual slalom riders, who need an abundance of muscle power in order to ply their trade.

Plyometric training is based on the principle that a concentric (shortening) muscle contraction is far greater than normal if it immediately follows an eccentric (lengthening) contraction. This is often illustrated using the analogy of a spring. If a spring is stretched it gives a far greater contraction force than if it is not. The same applies to muscles.

Plyometric exercises are easy to do and require little in the way of specialised training equipment.

The Workouts
DEPTH JUMP

Purpose: The most widely used plyometric exercise is the depth jump. This basic exercise develops leg power and enhances the contractile properties of the quadriceps muscle.

Procedure: In order to perform the depth jump you will need a sturdy box or bench (anywhere between 40 and 100 cm). Stand on top of the bench and drop down, landing either double or single footed. Bending your knees to absorb the shock causes the quadriceps muscles to quickly lengthen. You now need to contract these muscles as quickly and as powerfully as you can. In order to do this, upon landing, you should immediately jump up, exploding as high as possible. The key word here is immediately. As soon as you touch the floor you should instantly begin your explosive jump upwards.

Workout tips: To gain maximum benefit from this exercise you should be aiming to spend as little time as possible in contact with the ground.

If you are a beginner, start out performing two-footed landings. As you progress and become stronger, you can overload further by performing single-footed landings. If you are doing single-footed depth jumps, use a low bench in order to avoid injury.

Plyometric exercises enhance both strength and speed characteristics of muscular contraction and it is possible to place emphasis on either one or the other. The higher you drop down, the longer you will be in contact with the ground. This develops the strength component, whereas a lower height will minimise ground contact time and will develop the speed component more.

Bounding

PURPOSE: This is another classic plyometric exercise that is applicable to mountain biking. The purpose of this exercise is similar to that of depth jumps: to develop leg power and enhance the contractile properties of the quadriceps muscle.

PROCEDURE: In order to perform this exercise correctly and reduce the likelihood of injury you will need to use a flat, relatively soft surface such as grass or a running track. Mark out a start and finish area about 20 metres apart. From the start, perform two-footed bounds towards the finish. Aim to complete the distance with the minimum number of bounds. As with depth jumps, you should try to minimise your contact with the ground. As soon as you land you should be initiating your next bound.

WORKOUT TIPS: To gain maximum benefit from this exercise, you should be aiming to spend as little time as possible in contact with the ground.

If you are a beginner, start out performing two-footed bounds. Then as you progress and become stronger, you can perform single-footed bounds by taking a series of huge lunging strides.

Due to the intense nature of plyometrics, it is important that you act conservatively at all times. Ensure that you wear quality footwear with good shock absorption in the soles, and that you can get good purchase on the ground. The risk of injury is higher than in most other forms of exercise, so warm up, start off easy and gradually build up. A starter session for the above plyometric exercises is as follows:

> Depth Jumps: 3 x 8 jumps
> Bounding: 3 x 20m of bounding

In between sets it is important that you rest. Give yourself at least 30 seconds' rest between each set, more if you think you need it. Tired muscles will not only respond less to the exercises in a power sense, but they may also contribute to a lack of form which may lead to injury.

As with all other forms of exercise, it is important to remember that you are a mountain biker and that although leg power is a valuable asset it should not dominate your training. When you incorporate this workout into your programme, I suggest that you substitute one weight-training session with plyometrics.

8. PUTTING IT ALL TOGETHER

THE THEORY OF PERIODISATION AND SCHEDULING

So far we have examined the specific training workouts that you can use in order to elicit a training response in a specific area of your fitness. For these workouts to be effective they need to be orchestrated into a training schedule. Reaching peak fitness at the right time is one of the most difficult aspects of training to perfect. To be consistently in top form for a specific event, or series, year in year out, like the professionals are, is no accident. It takes them years of learning, careful documentation and analysis of different exercise schedules in order for them fully to understand and hone their fitness to a peak at the right time.

Every individual is different and as such no hard or fast blueprint exists for guaranteed peak preparation. All is not lost, however, as much research has been conducted in this area and a general pattern has emerged which should enable you to arrive at peak fitness at the right time.

Mountain bike events are externally fixed dates and unfortunately they cannot be rescheduled to suit your fitness status. The only option available is to manipulate your fitness to meet the external demands of the race. The best way to do this is via periodisation, as this provides a focus for your training and brings your fitness components to a peak at the right time.

Periodisation involves splitting the year up into sequential training blocks. The blocks are progressive and are designed to bring the rider to peak fitness for a predetermined point in time. Most top mountain bikers work on a 12-month schedule, with a view to reaching top form during the race season and then maintaining it for as long as possible. You should allow at least 20 to 28 weeks for training before the race season, about 20 weeks for your race season (during which you will be able to peak for a cumulative total of between 4 and 6 weeks), and up to 4 weeks' recovery following your peak. That is a 52-week cycle in total.

For this reason, I will be using a yearly cyclical programme as an example, but you can peak more than once in a year if you so wish. It is important to note that the more frequently you peak the more diminished it will be and the probability of over-training will increase many fold.

A cyclical training programme is one that continually repeats itself with each complete cycle called a 'macrocycle'. The typical mountain biking macrocycle contrasts with the calendar year by starting in the autumn. This allows enough time to reach peak fitness for the competition period which characteristically runs from April through to September. However, if your goal is to compete in a winter series then the principle of periodisation still applies; you will just have shift your training phases accordingly. The macrocycle is subdivided into 'mesocycles', each of which has a specific focus. These are then further divided into 'microcycles' or training weeks.

The number of microcycles in a mesocycle is dependent on the areas of fitness that you are focusing on. Some mesocycles are lengthy in order to allow particular fitness components, such as the cardiovascular system, to fully develop, whilst others are relatively short in duration because they are too intense to be included over a prolonged period without fear of over-training.

Included in the description of each mesocycle are examples of training programmes for both cross-country and downhill disciplines. Initially you can use them as a template to get you started, but as you progress you must tailor your programme to suit your own specific needs and weaknesses.

PHASES MAKING UP THE TRAINING YEAR

Diagram 9: The Mountain Bike Macrocycle

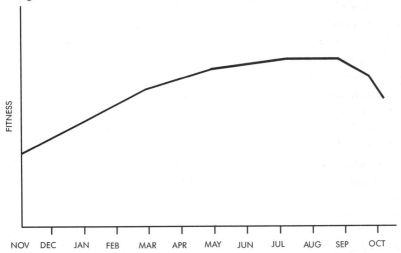

FOUNDATION	PREP 1	PREP 2	RACE SEASON	REST	MESOCYCLES
WEEKS 1 TO 9	10 TO 19	20 TO 29	30 TO 47	48 TO 52	MICROCYCLES

Table 7: The Components of Periodisation

	FOUNDATION	PREP 1	PREP 2	RACE (INC. PEAK)	RECOVERY
DURATION	8–10 weeks	8–10 weeks	8–10 weeks	18–20 weeks inc. 4–6 week peak	4–6 weeks
TRAINING MODE	– off-road – road cycling – running – aerobic cross-training – general sports – technique – resistance trainer	– off-road – road cycling – running – aerobic cross-training – general sports – technique – resistance trainer	– off-road – road cycling – running – aerobic cross-training – technique – strength – resistance trainer	– off-road – road cycling – technique – strength – resistance trainer – racing	– easy light exercise that is enjoyable
TRAINING TYPE	– continuous	– continuous – fartlek – intervals	– continuous – fartlek – intervals	– continuous – fartlek – intervals	– continuous
WORKOUTS	ModTI AeTI SSTI	ModTI AeTI SSTI AP AnTI	ModTI AeTI SSTI AP AnTI MaxTI	ModTI AeTI SSTI AP AnTI MaxTI	ModTI AeTI
PURPOSE	– build base endurance – develop & improve technique	– improve base endurance & develop overall strength – improve technique	– maintain endurance & strength – develop leg power – improve technique – bring all components to a simultaneous peak	– develop peak fitness	– recovery

Foundation Phase

Each new macrocycle begins with developing a base for the rest of the phases to build on. The foundation phase should commence with a battery of fitness tests in order to assess your initial fitness status. The training in the foundation phase is geared to developing your raw fitness which you will subsequently hone and peak for the summer racing. This phase should last for about eight to ten weeks and be skewed towards developing both a solid endurance and a strength base. It also prepares the body for the ensuing phases and will get you back into a training state of mind following the rest and recovery break. A temptation is to underestimate this phase and try to hurry it up by moving onto the more intense training prematurely. Hang fire, for the point to remember here is that training is like a pyramid: the broader the base, the higher the peak you can build. Put the time and effort in at the foundation phase and you will have your highest possible physical peak during the race season.

Diagram 10: Peaking

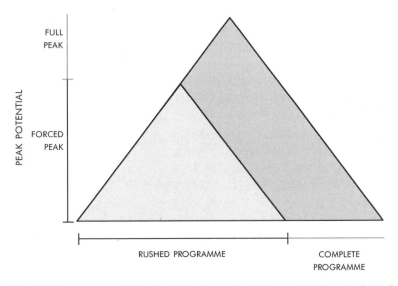

The bulk of your training in this phase should be centred around Moderate Training Intensity (ModTI), Aerobic Training Intensity (AeTI) and Steady State Training Intensity (SSTI) workouts. You should aim to include two high-rep strength workouts per week (no plyometrics at this stage) and a fartlek workout containing some easy climbing. Although you need to initiate a structure into your weekly training, your schedule shouldn't be too rigid at this stage. The race season is still a long time off and it is important not to get too bogged down with training regimes this early on. You need to maintain motivation and have fun, otherwise your enthusiasm will wane several months down the line and your fitness will suffer. You should try to avoid repetitive training by including a lot of cross-training in to this phase. Cross-training involves performing other endurance sports with the aim of improving your base endurance fitness. It also gives your mountain biking muscles a break and prevents you going stale both physically and mentally. For more information on cross-training see chapter thirteen.

Table 8: Cross-country Foundation Phase

MONDAY	Recovery; flexibility (30 minutes)
TUESDAY	1 hour fartlek; strength training (general conditioning)
WEDNESDAY	2 hours endurance ride or cross-training (SSTI)
THURSDAY	30 minutes active recovery (ModTI); flexibility (30 minutes)
FRIDAY	1 hour fartlek (cross-training)
SATURDAY	Strength training (general conditioning); 1 hour endurance cross-training (AeTI)
SUNDAY	2 hours endurance ride (SSTI)

Table 9: Downhill Foundation Phase

MONDAY	Anaerobic threshold workout 1
TUESDAY	1 hour fartlek (cross-training); strength training (general conditioning)
WEDNESDAY	30 minutes flexibility
THURSDAY	Strength training (general conditioning); 1 hour endurance ride (AeTI) or cross-training
FRIDAY	Anaerobic threshold workout 2
SATURDAY	1 hour fartlek; skill work
SUNDAY	2 hours endurance ride (SSTI)

More often than not, the foundation phase will take you through the autumn and early winter months when the chances of catching a cold or illness are heightened. Should you fall ill during this phase, reduce your training volume (to nil if necessary) and only continue with the full programme when you're completely recovered. It is inevitable that we all fall victim to illnesses at some time or other, but there are several actions that you can take in order to reduce the chances to a bare minimum:

1. Bolster your immune system by taking Echinacea. Echinacea is available in tablet form, but is far better when drunk as a tea mixed with a spoonful of honey. Echinacea teas are widely available at all good health food stores.
2. Eat a well-balanced diet and ensure that you are getting enough vitamins and

minerals by consuming plenty of fresh fruit and vegetables. Vitamin C and zinc supplementation has been shown to reduce the severity of colds, but you must catch the cold early for them to have a significant effect.

3. Make sure that you get plenty of sleep. You will need adequate recovery time during this training phase. Any shortcomings with regard to sleep can quickly accumulate and leave you an easy target for illness.

4. Make sure that you eat adequate carbohydrates (see chapter fifteen), as studies have shown that they can reduce the effects of the stress hormones associated with daily life and exercise and thus maintain the strength of your immune system.

5. Try to avoid people who are coughing and spluttering, especially during the high-risk period immediately after you have been training. As an extra precaution get into the habit of washing your hands regularly, as viruses can easily enter the body after you have touched something that is infected.

6. Don't worry about your weight during this period. Rapid weight loss can place a significant drain on the immune system.

7. Work in conjunction with the competing stresses in your life. Wherever possible shun stressful situations and maintain a good, regular training schedule. However, some life stresses are unavoidable and you should reduce your training intensity accordingly. This enables you to accommodate the new stresses and avoid placing too much strain on your immune system.

If you do become ill, all is not lost. As a rule of thumb, if your illness is above your chest – for example as a sore throat or runny nose – then you can test the water by training in the ModTI and the AeTI zones for several minutes. If they clear and your condition improves, you should be okay to continue training, albeit at a lower intensity. If your condition deteriorates, or your symptoms are in your chest, then you should avoid training and seek medical advice. It is foolish to 'push on' at all costs: this will have catastrophic repercussions later on in the macrocycle.

Preparation Phase One (P1)

This phase typically starts around January and should last anywhere between eight and ten weeks. As with the preceding phase, it is important to commence the P1 phase with the same battery of fitness tests in order to review your improvements and highlight key areas that still need work. The training emphasis during this phase is a gradual shift from cross-training to mountain biking. Only at the end of this phase should the volume of time spent training on your mountain bike supersede that spent cross-training. During this period you should also train in the AP and AnTI zones in addition to the ModTI, AeTI and the SSTI that you started in the foundation phase. Towards the end of the P1 phase is an appropriate time to schedule a training camp and focus upon your mountain biking. The training camp should last from one to two weeks and comprise a lot of high-volume work.

This is a relatively demanding training phase, especially if you have included a training camp, and as such it is important to incorporate at least one recovery week in order to allow your body the time to supercompensate and adapt fully to the new strains that you are placing upon it.

Table 10: Example Cross-country Prep Phase One

MONDAY	Rest; 30 minutes flexibility
TUESDAY	2 hours endurance ride (SSTI) with hollow sprints (AnTI)
WEDNESDAY	1 hour fartlek (ModTI–AeTI); plyometrics
THURSDAY	Anaerobic threshold workout 2 (AnTI)
FRIDAY	Rest; 30 minutes flexibility
SATURDAY	Strength training – power and strength; anaerobic threshold workout 1 (AnTI)
SUNDAY	2 hours endurance ride (SSTI/AeTI) with climbing intervals (AnTI)

Table 11: Example Downhill Prep Phase One

MONDAY	Anaerobic threshold workout 1 (AnTI)
TUESDAY	Strength training – power and strength; 30 minutes flexibility
WEDNESDAY	1 hour fartlek (ModTI–AeTI); plyometrics
THURSDAY	1½ hours fartlek (ModTI–AeTI) with long sprints (AnTI)
FRIDAY	Rest; 30 minutes flexibility
SATURDAY	2 hours endurance ride (SSTI/AP) with hollow sprints (AnTI)
SUNDAY	Strength training – power and strength; 1 hour endurance ride (AeTI)

Preparation Phase Two (P2)

This phase has a duration of 8 to 10 weeks, and depending upon your race season it will usually take you from March through to late April or mid-May. Once again, the full battery of fitness tests must be repeated at the start of the phase and you should review your progress to date. The sole purpose of this phase is to bring all of the components of your mountain bike fitness to a simultaneous peak for your racing schedule.

In terms of training volume and intensity, this is the hardest of all of the training phases. You should add MaxTI workouts to your repertoire of training and test your fitness by entering a race that you consider to be of lesser importance than your key races, but nonetheless is of sufficient standard to be a useful